JEREMY
CORBYN–
ACCIDENTAL HERO

'This biography by the new small publishing
house Eyewear Publishing will surely remain exceptional ...
Gilbert makes no bones about his admiration for Corbyn
but that hasn't misled him into writing a hagiographic tract
... [he] demolishes Corbyn's detractors with aplomb.
He's well informed about political history, he has
an easy and witty style and a keen perception
of what is central to the Corbyn phenomenon'.
– *Morning Star*

SQUINT

BRIEF BOOKS FOR A BUSY WORLD

Look More Closely

JEREMY
CORBYN—
ACCIDENTAL HERO

W STEPHEN GILBERT

EYEWEAR PUBLISHING

Second edition with new afterword
First published in 2015
by Eyewear Publishing Ltd
Suite 333, 19-21 Crawford Street
Marylebone, London W1H 1PJ
United Kingdom

Typeset with graphic design by Edwin Smet
Author photograph by Barbra Flinder
Corbyn picture with microphone RevolutionBahrainMC on YouTube *(Creative Commons license)*
Printed in England by TJ International Ltd, Padstow, Cornwall

ISBN 978-1-908998-97-2

Eyewear wishes to thank Jonathan Wonham for his very generous patronage of our press; as well as our other patrons and investors who wish to remain anonymous.

MIX
Paper from
responsible sources
FSC® C013056

WWW.EYEWEARPUBLISHING.COM

for Tony Coult

CONTENTS

LEADERS of the LABOUR PARTY

Keir Hardie 1906-08

Arthur Henderson 1908-10, 1914-17, 1931-32

George Barnes 1910-11

Ramsay MacDonald 1911-14, 1922-31 *(Prime Minister 1924, 1929-35; MacDonald surrendered party leadership during the latter years of his premiership)*

William Adamson 1917-21

JR Clynes 1921-22

George Lansbury 1932-35

Clement Attlee 1935-55 *(Prime Minister 1945-51)*

Hugh Gaitskell 1955-63 *(died in office)*

George Brown (acting) 1963

Harold Wilson 1963-76 *(Prime Minister 1964-70, 1974-76)*

James Callaghan 1976-80 *(Prime Minister 1976-79)*

Michael Foot 1980-83

Neil Kinnock 1983-92

John Smith 1992-94 *(died in office)*

Margaret Beckett (acting) 1994

Tony Blair 1994-2007 *(Prime Minister 1997-2007)*

Gordon Brown 2007-10 *(Prime Minister 2007-10)*

Harriet Harman (acting) 2010, 2015

Ed Miliband 2010-15

Jeremy Corbyn 2015-

INTRODUCTION FROM THE EDITOR

Squint is a new series from the British indie press, Eyewear Publishing, which aims to briefly look at and into issues and subjects of interest in the new digital age we are located in. Welcome to our first book (updated now to also explore he excitement of the last few weeks of 2015 and early 2016).

'Jeremy Corbyn –Threat Or Menace?'

That might well have been a headline over the past few months, if the infamous editor-in-chief and publisher from *Spider-Man*, J. Jonah Jameson, had been running a paper in the UK. Few if any recent political figures in British history have risen from relative obscurity so quickly, and been received with such equal measures of scorn and popular support. Will he push the so-called nuclear button? Does he ever sing the national anthem? Is he really friends with *those* people? Questions abound.

On a personal note, I met Mr Corbyn back in 2003, at a poetry launch on Betterton Street. The MP was both generous and helpful in introducing an anthology I had edited then, *100 Poets Against The War*. He briefly spoke about his opposition to what he felt was the illegal war that Blair and other Labour grandees were prosecuting. And when the reading was over, he left, as quietly and modestly as he had come in. I have not met Mr Corbyn since, and, to be honest, he soon slipped out of my mind, as yet one more minor political figure on the fringes of things.

Well, now he is back, no longer on the fringes, and, whatever transpires, he will remain unforgettable, at worst a famous footnote in history, at best, a genuine game-changer. Either way, I am proud to have published this book at this crucial time, for him, and for Britain.

We at Eyewear admit to finding Mr Corbyn fascinating, and some of his ideas and objectives invigorating, which is why we chose to inaugurate our series with a study of the man, the myth, his ideas and actions, from birth to the end of his first months as Leader of the Labour Party. Writing to a tight deadline, and driven by a sense of duty and wit, Mr Gilbert has produced a readable, lively, and even entertaining book that, only six months ago, would not have made sense to commission or create. A week is indeed a long time in politics, and an aeon in publishing.

Our staff – many of them in their 20s and early 30s – find Mr Corbyn a breath of fresh air. When we at Eyewear wanted to know more, about his actual life story, and what he really thinks and means to do with his new prominence, we found it hard to locate, in any one handy guide, the information we needed.

You have that guide here, now, in your hands. It is bound to divide opinion, perhaps even be seen in some quarters as controversial or polemical. No contemporary introduction to a politician like Corbyn could expect less than a turbulent reception, because the man and his ideas do, often, upset the apple cart of received establishment opinion. The reason he excited so many and got them to support his leadership campaign is the same reason that, now he is Leader of the Labour Party, he seems dangerous to others. In his own way, he is as radical as a Cromwell or a Thatcher. If he ever became Prime Minister, Britain would change, of that we can be sure.

Todd Swift
Director of Eyewear Publishing Ltd

London, UK
19 October, 2015
17 February, 2016, new edition

PREFACE

There was once a land where the political class had grown very unpopular. People said that the politicians were all the same, that they spoke double-talk and they were just out for themselves. One party, which had changed a lot over a quarter of a century, had lost two elections in a row and sought a new leader. A man came along who wanted to take the party back to its core values and who spoke clearly and evinced no personal ambition. He had an extraordinarily galvanising effect, enthusing young people (even though he was old) who had been alienated from politics for a long time and bringing back to the party many who had left in dismay. Those who reckon to measure these things found that his popularity far outstripped that of his rivals. But the party's hierarchy said that he was 'unelectable', even though his majority in his own constituency was enormous, and so they did their best to bring his progress to a halt.

Of course, this must be a fairy story. It is too absurd to be credible in the real world.

I wrote that in early August 2015, when the campaign for the leadership of the Labour Party in Britain was in full swing and it was clear that Jeremy Corbyn was ahead of his three rivals. I sent it as a 'letter to the editor' to *The Guardian* newspaper but it wasn't published. *The Guardian* didn't get it and they continued not to get it. The headline to one comment piece – "Wake up, unions: there will be no Prime Minister Corbyn"[1] – irresistibly echoed the famous *Daily Express* headline of August 1939: "There will be no war". I imagine this was inadvertent rather than deliberate.

Nor did the rest of the British press get it. All the papers editorially endorsed runners other than Corbyn (*The Guardian* chose Yvette Cooper), save for the *Morning Star* (where Corbyn has a column) and the Glasgow-based, Labour-supporting *Daily Record*. Among proprietors, the exception was Rupert Murdoch of News International who tweeted: "Corbyn increasingly likely Labor [*sic*] winner. Seems only candidate who believes anything, right or wrong"[2]. This was met with general astonishment, but not among those of us who have noted that Murdoch only ever backs winners.

Politicians' relationships with the press are always a matter of interest and controversy. The

1 August 7th 2015
2 Twitter [August 19th 2015]

distance between Westminster and what was then still called Fleet Street[3] was considerably shortened throughout the 1980s by Margaret Thatcher who, having been discounted by the press when a candidate for the Tory leadership, determined to recruit its denizens as allies. Not only did she cultivate proprietors, editors and political correspondents, she also sprinkled honours over them: David English of the *Daily Mail*, Larry Lamb of *The Sun* and Nicholas Lloyd of the *Daily Express* were all knighted and Bill Deedes of *The Daily Telegraph* was raised to the peerage by Thatcher; Peregrine Worsthorne of *The Sunday Telegraph* was knighted by Thatcher's successor, John Major.

As a foreign national (Australian born, US naturalised), Murdoch could not be knighted or ennobled but his interests could be greatly assisted. Thatcher saw that Murdoch met no hitch in his intent to buy *The Times* and *The Sunday Times*, the most ticklish of which would be reference to the Monopolies and Mergers Commission. In taking over these titles, Murdoch undertook to maintain their independence. Readers will have their views on how far he kept that promise.

3 For decades Fleet Street, which runs from St Clement Danes to Ludgate, was the main thoroughfare of London's newspaper district, most of the national titles being sited on or near it. However, in the 1980s all the publishers relocated. (Uniquely, DC Thomson, Dundee-based publisher of legendary comics, still has its London office in Fleet Street)

The union of Thatcher's political and Murdoch's business interests was dramatised in the year-long dispute over new technology and workers' rights at News International's printing plant at Wapping (1986-87), which eventually broke the print union and emboldened Thatcher in her overhauling of all industrial relations.

During the time that Thatcher was in office, the Murdoch press began to account for one third of all daily and Sunday copy sales in Britain and hence became a major influence on public opinion. Using his titles, especially *The Sun*, Murdoch made his support for particular politicians and policies crystal clear. Part of the unspoken deal was that these politicians took notice of his influence. Under John Major, the support that Murdoch offered began to wane, partly because Major was an enthusiast for the European Union about which both Thatcher and Murdoch were far more scornful, partly because Major's instincts were not to cosy up to proprietors and editors to the same degree.

After successive Labour leaders had failed to dislodge Thatcher or Major from office, former barrister Tony Blair was elected as a telegenic moderniser who shunned the term 'socialist' and sought to argue that Labour bore business and high finance no ill-will. He was as eager as Thatcher to cultivate the Tory press. His targets were Lord Rothermere, owner of the *Daily Mail*; Conrad Black, then owner of the *Telegraph* group (whom Blair raised to the peerage and had first met through the Bilderberg Conferences[4] that he – Blair – flatly denied attending); and particularly Murdoch[5]. Blair even became godfather to one of the children born of Murdoch's third wife, Wendi Deng. And Blair, though a relative Europhile, looked a winner as Major increasingly looked a loser.

The British press is broadly Tory-supporting, being mostly owned by tax-exiled billionaires who fiercely dislike even mildly progressive Labour policies. The BBC and other broadcasters, charter-bound to be neutral in terms of party, are seen as supportive of the status quo, however it might be cast at the time – over warfare, for instance. Led by Murdoch, the right-wing press gave Blair an easy ride, even when he joined President George W Bush in prosecuting (against the Iraqi regime) a war that was widely thought to be illicit if not downright illegal.

Murdoch had no compunction about instructing his editors to undermine the reputations of Michael

4 These are annual meetings of like-minded industrialists, financiers and politicians. Members have included Edward Heath, Thatcher, Blair, Gordon Brown and David Cameron, Gerald Ford, Henry Kissinger, Bill and Hillary Clinton, Colin Powell, Condoleeza Rice, John Kerry, Bill Gates, Ben Bernanke, Princes Philip and Charles, and Bernhard of the Netherlands, and so on

5 Blair also knighted Max Hastings, retiring editor of the *Evening Standard*

Foot and Neil Kinnock, successive leaders of the Labour Party during Thatcher's and Major's terms of office, nor of the Tory leaders that faced Blair when the Conservatives were in opposition (William Hague, Iain Duncan Smith and, to a rather lesser extent, Michael Howard who still failed to defeat Blair at a general election). By the time that Blair stepped down and handed the premiership on to Gordon Brown, Murdoch had lost patience with Labour and, even though Brown courted him as energetically as Blair had done, the press generally turned against Labour and embraced David Cameron instead, though never with great enthusiasm as his stance on Europe was thought to be unstable.

After Brown's defeat in the general election of 2010, his Labour successor was anathema to the Tory press. Ed Miliband was initially seen as dangerously left-wing and the papers dubbed him "Red Ed". But Labour's positions wavered during its opposition to the coalition government led by Cameron's Tories. On certain issues, like press regulation and tax avoidance, Miliband took bold stances at the risk of alienating press proprietors more personally than most. And he was ferociously undermined for it.

Much of the assault had an unpleasant

undertone, one that was never deployed against a previous opposition leader who was also Jewish, Michael Howard. Miliband's late father Ralph, a Marxist intellectual of Polish descent, was accounted in the *Daily Mail* "the man who hated Britain"[6], despite his three years in the Royal Navy during World War II; *Mail* editor Paul Dacre's father Peter had avoided war service through a connection with Lord Beaverbrook, then proprietor of the *Daily Express* and a government minister.

Miliband's nasal voice and his alleged 'weirdness' were mocked. He was characterised as having "stabbed his brother in the back" because he ran successfully against David Miliband (and three others) for leadership of the Labour Party. And although every figure in public life suffers unflattering photographs on a daily basis, very few of such shots are ever published. But Ed Miliband was scorned for weeks over a particularly unfortunate image, as though it must somehow be his own fault that he could not look like George Clooney from every angle at every moment. The image was even trotted out again on the front page of Murdoch's *The Sun* on the morning of the 2015 election to clinch Miliband's supposed unsuitability for office or 'unelectability'.

This is the level of opposition, of vilification,

6 September 27th 2013

misrepresentation and spite that Corbyn knows he faces as leader of the opposition. He will need broad shoulders and a thick skin. From the moment his leadership campaign started to gain traction, it seemed much of the press was out to discredit him, greatly assisted by many leading members of the Labour Party itself, who take the view sincerely or affect the view tactically that Labour cannot win a general election with Corbyn as leader. Well, we shall see.

CHAPTER 1: UNDETECTABLE

So who is this man who rose without trace to lead Britain's Labour Party? Christened Jeremy Bernard Corbyn, he was born the youngest of four brothers on May 26th 1949 in Chippenham in the western English county of Wiltshire. Based on a settlement at least two millennia old, Chippenham is situated on the river Avon equidistantly between Bath to the west and Royal Wootton Bassett to the east. It was an evacuee town during World War II and also a Luftwaffe target, doubtless because the Westinghouse Brake and Signal Company, an important supplier of engineering work, was the main employer in the area. Until the mid-1950s, though, Chippenham was primarily a pleasant market town. Since then, the population has been tripled, largely by the development of housing estates. The local youth tend to refer to the town as 'Nam.

Jeremy's mother Naomi was a teacher of maths to girls, no doubt an enterprise looked at askance by quite a lot of men in the Britain of the 1940s.

His father David worked at Westinghouse as an electrical engineer. They met through campaigning for peace, specifically peace in Spain – it was the time of the Spanish Civil War. David and Naomi Corbyn lived in the village of Kington St Michael, a little way outside Chippenham.

The Corbyn family were of a sort much encountered in the West Country: middle class non-conformists. Dissent has a long history across the west, particularly expressed through independent and renegade versions of theology and worship, but also in literature and thought: the Devon-born poet and pamphleteer Samuel Taylor Coleridge made his home in Somerset. Non-conformism was still being expressed in recent decades by the relatively high incidence of Liberal Democrat MPs being elected in what is otherwise a Conservative-voting region. At the 2015 election though, all Lib Dem representation in the west was eliminated and Labour only held onto the seat of Exeter.

As well as the liberal tradition, the Labour left has old connections with the west. Michael Foot was born in Plymouth in Devon, where his father became Lord Mayor after serving as Liberal MP for Bodmin, Cornwall. Tony Benn became Bristol South East MP – at 25 in 1950 – after Sir Stafford Cripps stood down. Benn fought a famous battle to stay in the seat after inheriting his father's title of Viscount Stansgate, becoming the first to renounce a peerage.

When Jeremy was seven, the Corbyns moved 100 miles north to the tiny village of Pave Lane near Newport in Shropshire. David Corbyn had stayed at the guesthouse established in an old manor in the village and he liked the place so much that he bought it. With seven bedrooms, it was a good base for a family of six. While his siblings pursued technical interests – meteorology, geology, aerodynamics (brother Edward worked on the Concorde's design) – Jeremy explored the surrounding countryside and books. At home, he constructed a sundial, installed in the garden. These enthusiasms have stayed with him. He has long worked an allotment in Thatcher's old parliamentary constituency of Finchley.

The brothers all attended Adams' Grammar School in Newport, one of the most highly rated schools in the state system. Here Jeremy parts ways with Foot and Benn who were both educated in the independent sector. As a teenager, having imbibed the family taste for political debate, he joined the League Against Cruel Sports, which campaigns to end all versions of hunting, and became a member of the Young Socialists in the local constituency (The Wrekin), a classic marginal seat for many decades but getting safer for the Conservatives over the last ten years, having been rendered more rural by boundary changes.

After school, Corbyn taught for two years in Jamaica as part of the Voluntary Service Overseas scheme, then still in its first decade of operation. On his return he took successive jobs in trade unions (the National Union of Public Employees and the National Union of Tailors and Garment Workers, both defunct), an administrative post in the National Health Service and an unfinished further education course, before diving into elective London politics, first as a local councillor in Haringey (where he met Jane Chapman, his first wife), then in 1983 at age 34, entering parliament as the member for Islington North. That same year he was offered the column in the *Morning Star* that he has contributed ever since.

So into the Commons came a most atypical new member. He was remarkably abstemious if not quite teetotal. He was a vegetarian by conviction. He and Jane had crossed Europe several times by motorcycle. Later they would amicably go their separate ways. He married twice more, divorcing the Chilean mother of his sons when her ambition to get the boys into a grammar school beyond their catchment area led to an irreconcilable split.

His third wife is Mexican by birth and he speaks fluent Spanish. His favourite eating-place is kosher: Gaby's Deli in the Charing Cross Road. He has always had an educated interest in literature, citing WB Yeats and Chinua Achebe as particular enthusiasms. Irish novelist Ronan Bennett once worked on his Westminster staff. He writes his own verse, strictly for private consumption, and paints abstracts. He is almost certainly the first leadership candidate in any party to include in his manifesto a coherent arts policy. I feel quite sure that Margaret Thatcher didn't do that.

"He loves making jam with fruit grown on his allotment, belongs to the All Party Parliamentary Group for Cheese and is a train obsessive" according to Jim Pickard[7]. By his own account, his headteacher's parting comment to him was: "You will not make anything of yourself"[8].

A non-driver, Corbyn shares with both David Cameron and Boris Johnson a devotion to cycling. He will no doubt have to abandon cycling in London, as Cameron has done: security will not permit it. Whether he would turn down the Jaguar XJ ministerial saloons that go with government office we may see in 2020. Maybe he will favour a

---

7 *Financial Times* [July 23rd 2015]
8 Quoted in *The Daily Telegraph* [September 12th 2015]

Fiat 500, like the Pope on his official visit to the White House. He also runs, is avid about cricket and follows Arsenal FC.

He is famously frugal, "the only man I know who buys his clothes at the Dalston Co-op" as one Islington activist twitted him[9]. And here's something that all those who have grown cynical about politicians of all persuasions can and should cheer to the echo: in nearly every year that he has been in the House he was the member who claimed the lowest amount in expenses.

Corbyn's maiden speech, on July 1st 1983, set the tone for the 32 years of backbench recalcitrance to come: "[this House] seems a million miles away from the constituency that I represent and the problems that the people there face. Islington North is only a few miles from the House by tube or bus. We are suffering massive unemployment and massive cuts imposed by the Government on the local authorities.

"There are cuts in the Health Service. In common with the rest of inner London, we have lost all grant funding for education. That is a measure of the contempt with which the Government have treated Islington North – indeed, the whole borough of Islington[10]. The borough has suffered an

---

9 Quoted by Leo McKinstry in *The Daily Telegraph* [June 16th 2015]
10 It is a non-negotiable convention of the House that a maiden speech concentrates on the speaker's own constituency

unprecedented media attack in exactly the same way as the GLC[11] suffered because it was singled out as fair game for editorials in the *Daily Mail, The Sun* and other newspapers ...

"I represent an area of London that has suffered as much as any other from the policies of this Government, and I shall be telling the House repeatedly that we do not intend to take these issues lying down. We shall not allow unemployment to go through the roof. We shall not allow our youth to have no chance and no hope for the future. We shall not allow our borough councils to be attacked mercilessly in the way that they have been by the Government and by the press in the past year. We shall return to these issues because justice has to be done for those who are worst off and unemployed in areas such as the constituency that I represent"[12]. The reference to the GLC aside, Corbyn might have been addressing a rally in his 2015 campaign.

One of the qualities that particularly attracts supporters to Corbyn is that he speaks with

11 The Greater London Council was the elected body that administered the capital's governance. In every election since its inception in 1963 (replacing the London County Council), control of the GLC was won by the party in opposition in the Commons. It was generally perceived that it was almost entirely because the GLC was then led by Thatcher's fierce enemy and Corbyn's close friend and ally, Ken Livingstone, that the government was bent on abolishing it, which it duly did (with a tiny Commons majority in the vote) in 1986. Under the Blair government, an elected mayoralty was created for London and a new body, the Greater London Authority, was set up. Livingstone was installed as mayor by the voters and soon became as unwelcome to Blair as he had been to Thatcher
12 Hansard online [www.parliament.uk/business/publications/hansard]

unvarying and unwavering conviction. He is a signpost in Tony Benn's famous formula: "In politics there are weathercocks and signposts – weathercocks will spin in whatever direction the wind of public opinion may blow them, no matter what principle they may have to compromise. And there are signposts, signposts which stand true and tall and principled"[13].

Some also quote Emerson: "A foolish consistency is the hobgoblin of little minds, adored by little statesmen and philosophers and divines"[14]. Consistency, though, is considered essential in politics. Changes of view or policy, whether made self-critically in mature reflection and increased knowledge, or pragmatically in sober assessment of what the public will accept, need to be carefully prepared and skilfully presented. Andy Burnham's leadership campaign was damaged by a perception that his positions slid according to his audience and the tenor of the day, that in Benn's formula he was a weathercock. He was reportedly

13 I have failed to source this quote but it was revived by the new 'baby of the House', the SNP's Mhairi Black, in her inspirational maiden speech [July 14th 2015]

14 The passage continues: "With consistency a great soul has simply nothing to do. He may as well concern himself with his shadow on the wall. Speak what you think now in hard words, and to-morrow speak what to-morrow thinks in hard words again, though it contradict every thing you said to-day. — 'Ah, so you shall be sure to be misunderstood.' — Is it so bad, then, to be misunderstood? Pythagoras was misunderstood, and Socrates, and Jesus, and Luther, and Copernicus, and Galileo, and Newton, and every pure and wise spirit that ever took flesh. To be great is to be misunderstood". [Ralph Waldo Emerson, 'Self-Reliance' *Essays: First Series* 1841]

"agonising"[15] before taking a post under Corbyn. Corbyn doesn't do agonising.

Here is an interesting perspective that emerged nine years ago in a letter written in 1982 to the then Labour leader Michael Foot: "[Tony] Benn is in one sense quite right in saying that the right wing of the Party is politically bankrupt. Socialism ultimately must appeal to the better minds of the people. You cannot do that if you are tainted overmuch with a pragmatic period in power. The phrases that rouse us or should rouse us are bound to seem stale in the mouth of anyone who has been too closely intertwined with the establishment. It may not be fair but it is true"[16]. And who was the author of this candid assessment? The young Tony Blair. You may be sure no such letter has been written to Jeremy Corbyn.

An instinctive joiner, Corbyn the new MP immediately entered the six month-old Campaign Group of leftist MPs, an alliance that had been formed by Tony Benn, Stuart Holland, Joan Maynard, Dennis Canavan, Bob Cryer, Norman Atkinson and others out of a split in the Tribune Group. That 'soft left' alliance was named for the fortnightly magazine *Tribune* that was founded by Stafford Cripps and George Strauss in 1937 and

15 *The Observer* [September 13th 2015]
16 July 28th 1982, published in *The Daily Telegraph* and elsewhere [June 16th 2006]

edited during the war by Aneurin Bevan and on two later occasions by Michael Foot. After the split, the Tribune Group moved nearer to the mainstream.

In the Campaign Group, Corbyn was befriended by Benn and two others who still sit in the Commons with him, Michael Meacher and the so-called 'Beast of Bolsover', Dennis Skinner. Among current members are Diane Abbott and its chair, John McDonnell, but its heyday had looked to have passed; Corbyn's election may revive it or perhaps render it unnecessary.

Corbyn reminisced: "[when] I joined in 1983, it was a large organisation with 40 or 50 MPs. There were big discussions about economic policy, the miners' strike and foreign policy debates. In one hilarious meeting, the Greenham Women[17] addressed us. They were trying to buy bolt-cutters to cut the fences at Greenham Common, but any time they turned up at a shop anywhere near, they were denied the right to buy them. So each Campaign Group member agreed to buy one set of bolt-cutters and donate them to the Greenham Women. Which we duly did"[18].

17 An all-women peace camp was set up in autumn 1981 to maintain a vigil outside the wire mesh surrounding RAF Greenham Common in Berkshire, which was a storage site for nuclear warheads. In one form or another, the protest was kept going (sometimes fitfully) for almost two decades, by which time all missiles had been removed. The base was decommissioned in 1993
18 *Total Politics* website [June 28th 2011]

As a new MP in 1983, Corbyn found a Labour Party demoralised and embarking on a fifth year in opposition. A leader to succeed Michael Foot was elected four months after the general election. Neil Kinnock was regarded as being from the left of the party and his defeat of the centre-right candidate, Roy Hattersley, was comprehensive[19]. But Kinnock was soon embroiled in a power struggle with the left, many of whose adherents considered that he had moved right to gain party advancement.

The national miners' strike of 1984, which became a must-win issue for Thatcher, put Kinnock in a cleft stick. As MP for a mining constituency in Wales, he was sympathetic to their case against mine closures, but industrial action was always tricky for Labour leaders. Conservatives generally have the easier task of deploring and castigating "bolshie" workers and the "disruption to the public" that they cause. Labour's response, frequently compromised or – shall we say? – more nuanced, lends itself to derision and scorn.

What's more, Kinnock and the National Union of Mineworkers president Arthur Scargill simply loathed each other. Scargill had not made the move away from the left that Kinnock had effected. As the infamous leader of the legendary Yorkshire

19 At the result, Hattersley broke into the Howard Dietz/Arthur Schwartz song 'I Guess I'll Have to Change My Plan' which goes on "I should have known that there would be another man"

miners, he had played no small role in the 1974 miners' strike that provoked Edward Heath into fatally calling the general election that brought down his government. Ten years on and now the top man, Scargill sought to repeat the trick with Thatcher. Kinnock deplored his aims and his tactics.

A flashpoint of the strike was the so-called Battle of Orgreave. The NUM called a mass picket of the Orgreave coking plant but MI5 infiltration alerted South Yorkshire Police to the plan and the pickets were met with overwhelming force. There was a running battle for most of the day and many were injured on both sides including Scargill who was also arrested. Resentment against police tactics rumbled on for years; eventually the force were obliged to compensate 39 miners to the tune of half a million pounds. Miners had been assaulted without provocation and falsely arrested, and evidence fabricated. The same force was also indicted for its handling of the disaster at Hillsborough football ground five years after Orgreave and more recently blamed for its incompetence in investigating child abuse in Rotherham.

Long retired, Scargill spoke on the Orgreave Truth and Justice Campaign on September 17th

2015. Corbyn had been scheduled to attend too, but understandably in his first week as Labour leader he had to content himself with calling for an independent inquiry into Orgreave and demanding an apology from David Cameron for the Thatcher government's treatment of the miners, a demand inevitably scoffed at by the Prime Minister.

The miners' strike was a natural cause on which Corbyn could feel his way. In questions to the Leader of the House, the urbane John Biffen, on June 21st 1984, Corbyn alleged that the automobiles of NUM pickets "were being entered on the stolen vehicles index by the national police computer. Is not that an attempt to make all pickets into criminals, or at least to call them criminals, an example of the police state methods that are being used against the NUM, and yet another reason for an urgent debate on the future of the mining industry and ways to end the dispute?"

The parlaying of a slight, unsupported allegation into "police state methods" shows Corbyn already mastering the particular cadences of leftist rhetoric. Biffen duly flattered to deceive: "The point that the hon gentleman raises is a serious one, and I shall draw it to the attention of my right hon and learned friend the Home Secretary"[20].

20 Business of the House [TheyWorkForYou website] "Hon(ourable)" – to MPs generally – and "right hon" – to MPs who are members of the Privy Council that formally advises the monarch – are required forms of Commons address; "and learned" indicates a QC

Corbyn was one of many disgusted that the abused miners were obliged to wait to be exonerated. "If only the coverage now given to personal accounts of the strike and its hardships had been allowed ... in 1984-5" he said in 2014. "People ... seem to think that history is safe – it's only the present that's not"[21].

The government's moves to bring down the GLC and the ILEA[22] were a matter on which Corbyn was frequently exercised and was to find himself at odds with the Liberal MP Simon Hughes who, in one of the nastiest by-elections ever fought, had captured the Bermondsey seat and was to hold onto it until 2015[23]. In a debate on the GLC, Corbyn declared: "The hon Member for Southwark and Bermondsey made a remark about enterprise zones. I can think of nothing more insulting to the people of London, and especially to the nearly 500,000 Londoners without a job, than the idea of creating free enterprise zones to bring in a Hong Kong-style economy that allows people to grab all the money they can, make as much profit as they can, disregard the planning controls for which

21 Quoted in 'Mining the Meaning: The Legacy of the 1984-5 UK Miners' Strike' by Dr Katy Shaw, *The London Economic* [April 22nd 2014]

22 Inner London Education Authority, abolished in 1990

23 Labour MP Bob Mellish, disenchanted with Foot's leadership, resigned in February 1983. The Labour candidate was Peter Tatchell, later arguably Britain's most famous LGBT activist, though in fact never 'out' during the by-election campaign. The Liberals conducted a fierce whispering campaign, even though Hughes ("the straight choice") was himself an undeclared bisexual. Hughes was knighted after losing the seat in 2015

many of us have fought throughout the years, throw the workers on the scrap heap and then disappear to some other tax haven in some other part of the world. That is the reality of enterprise zones. If the hon Member for Southwark and Bermondsey supports them, perhaps he will tell the people of his constituency that he opposes planning controls and any form of normal democratic control over the ravages of private enterprise"[24].

What is most striking about Corbyn's record of speaking and putting down questions in his early days in parliament is how often he was drawn to foreign affairs. Central America generally, El Salvador, Nicaragua, Grenada, Cyprus, Turkey, Bangladesh, the World Bank and other global banks and the Commonwealth Heads of Government Meeting all prompted questions and speeches. Doubtless in a spirit of mischief, he asked in a written question if the Defence Secretary would submit to interrogation on the activities of "special forces" in overseas countries[25]. John Stanley's crisp rejoinder was "No"[26].

Those exercised by Corbyn's perceived views on women will be interested in a written request put to

---

24 Hansard: Debate on Greater London Council (Money Bill) [July 11th 1983]
25 The question was prompted, one imagines, by the formation in 1983 of a Special Task Force within the British Army's elite Special Air Service, which specialises in covert operations of surveillance and destabilisation
26 Hansard [July 12th 1983]

the Home Secretary three months later: "if, in view of the serious nature of the crime of rape and its effect on women victims, he will seek to establish firm procedures for the investigation of rape cases, after consultation with appropriate groups, which would include the following elements: (a) that police officers not implementing this procedure would be liable to disciplinary action, (b) that the woman victim is given the choice of being examined by a woman doctor as of right, (c) that all police officers are given training in this area to enable them to carry out questioning with tact and understanding, (d) that the woman should not be asked about the nature of her employment throughout the investigation, and (e) that the woman is given information about court procedures and possible referrals to other agencies". Douglas Hurd gave the customary fending-off type of answer that ministers of all parties offer[27].

From the foregoing, it may be seen that the young MP quickly found his feet, gamely challenging ministers and raising matters that many, no doubt including on his own side of the House, would prefer to be left alone. His style of addressing an audience was also established early and has evidently changed little over three decades. Not even his most devoted fan would

27 Hansard [October 24th 1983]

claim that the gift of great oratory is his. He is an artisan of rhetoric, lacking memorable, new-minted phraseology but usually strikingly sincere.

The left tradition that I have already invoked held public speaking in high regard. Aneurin Bevan was one of the very greatest. "That shit Bevan", declared Winston Churchill, no mean speechifier himself, "his phrases were dictated by some inner god"[28]. Bevan's successors Michael Foot and Tony Benn could each hold a crowd spellbound and frequently did. Enoch Powell, with his classicist's allusions and wintry cadences, was a vivid speaker in another part of the forest. Harold Macmillan, Jo Grimond, Anthony Crosland, Jeremy Thorpe, Roy Jenkins, Barbara Castle, Denis Healey, Michael Heseltine, Neil Kinnock, Robin Cook, Charles Kennedy, Vince Cable, Boris Johnson, Alan Johnson and Kenneth Clarke could deploy the great advantage of wit in rousing an audience and eloquently turning an argument.

But the great tradition of public speaking has greatly declined. Years ago, in a New York hotel room, I bumped into a stump speech by Senator Edward Kennedy broadcast on C-SPAN. Once joined, there was no leaving the programme until Kennedy was done. Electrifying doesn't come close. There are no speakers of that quality in British politics these days.

---

28 Quoted by Andrew Roberts, *The Daily Telegraph* [October 25th 2008]

Corbyn's speeches are solid and workaday. He makes heavy use of the old trick of grouping points into threes, delivered in identical forms: you saw it in that maiden speech and heard it again when he accepted the Labour leadership. He probably does not even notice that he does it, for it is second nature.

What is even more noticeable is that he speaks the same way for all audiences and all occasions. It is as though he is permanently in campaign mode. I have no knowledge as to how far he works with speechwriters, how far his words are his own, scribbled on late-night train journeys. Because he has no time for spin-doctors and – no doubt the same charlatans in his opinion – none for image advisors, debate coaches and policy wonks, his words come unvarnished and unpolished. There are fluffs and stumbles and mistimings and heedless remarks because he rejects a slick and professional attitude to performance and public appearance. The reluctant donning of a suit and tie for leadership appearances in the House and at functions is the most the public may expect. Will they respect his consistent lack of ingratiation or tire of it?

The nearest Corbyn does to jokes is jocularity. In his leadership acceptance speech, he generously and appropriately spoke to the individual strengths of his defeated rivals. The hardest one to praise, not surprisingly, was the diametrically opposed one, the Blairite Liz Kendall. Corbyn sensibly credited her for "standing up for what she believes in", but then mistimed and misconveyed a throwaway line – "those late-night train rides will never be the same again" – that fell dead on the platform.

Few politicians do comedy well. Heavily scripted and weightily delivered punchlines come across as passion-killers and then have to be manhandled and carried shoulder-high from the room by the speaker's claque. Watch again on YouTube Margaret Thatcher's mouthing of the line the playwright Ronald Millar[29] crafted for her in a conference speech in 1980: "the lady's not for turning". From the reaction of conference, you would think that Max Miller or Billy Connolly had suddenly stepped onto the platform.

Even in 1980, you'd have to have been at least fifty to get the 'joke'. *The Lady's Not for Burning* was a verse play by Christopher Fry (who went in for such things) that enjoyed a brief vogue at the start of the 1950s and then fell out of fashion and interest (as indeed did Fry who, rather surprisingly,

---

29 Like Christopher Fry, Millar was an actor-turned-minor-playwright. Cameron has his own in Julian Fellowes. Thatcher knighted Millar, Cameron ennobled Fellowes

lived into the 21st century and died at 97). Nothing in Thatcher's rendition of the line begins to suggest that she understood it. She must have allowed Tim Bell or some other lieutenant to persuade her that this was a telling remark to make. Well, poorly as she played it, we still speak of it.

Along with speeches in the House, addressing rallies of like-minded, uncritical enthusiasts is the kind of speaking that Corbyn has done most in his career. He has joined a number of political organisations that favour rallies and marches as their chief form of public expression. Corbyn was in the Campaign for Nuclear Disarmament at the age of 17; it is probably the forum in which he first encountered Arthur Scargill. CND was formed in 1957, its Easter marches to London from the Atomic Weapons Research Establishment at Aldermaston in Berkshire being something of a media event, especially when led by the distinguished, if widely-thought eccentric, philosopher, Bertrand Russell.

CND continues to agitate for unilateral nuclear disarmament, one of the platforms on which Corbyn, who remains among three CND vice-chairs, ran as Labour leader. I am no believer in the pseudo-science of opinion polling which can mislead as much by poorly chosen and worded questions as by never-explained "weighting" of the results. But a poll published in *The Guardian* found opposition to the renewal of Trident as high as 79 per cent, an impressive figure[30]. This is another Corbyn position dismissed as extreme but which, like renationalisation of the railways, the power companies and the Post Office, seems to command wide public support.

Professor Paul Rogers argues with "the assumption that opposing Trident renewal is a vote loser. In reality that may have been the case a few years ago, but a new generation has emerged and it is far from clear that it is any longer a key issue. The idea that international standing depends on being able to kill five million people in 45 minutes has much less traction than it did, and the huge cost of a Trident replacement, at a time of supposed austerity, is another factor that will be easy for Corbyn to highlight"[31].

As the Trident missile system, based to the Scottish government's chagrin at Faslane above the Firth of Clyde, comes up for replacement in 2016, the potential for deep division in the Labour Party is enormous. Some members of the shadow cabinet – Lord Falconer (justice) and Hilary Benn (foreign affairs) among them – have said that Trident is a "red line issue" for them.

---

30 April 8th 2014
31 *The Independent* [August 22nd 2015]

David Cameron is committed to maintaining Trident in its current form as a continuous-at-sea missile system, at a cost of £3 billion per year. Ed Miliband went into the 2015 election with Labour prepared to scale back Trident from its present four submarines to three, a policy echoed by Nick Clegg's Liberal Democrats though, in the Lib Dems' case, with the option of further reductions. The ruling Scottish Nationalist Party, the Green Party and the United Kingdom Independence Party all proposed to scrap Trident; but Nigel Farage of UKIP uniquely advocated a "cheaper" replacement system launched from land or air as well as sea[32].

Labour's position on Britain's nuclear capability is not the only one changing. Chancellor George Osborne revealed at the end of August 2015 that he had contracted half-a-billion pounds of support services at Faslane. Scotland's First Minister, Nicola Sturgeon, called this "an arrogant decision by the Chancellor to try to pre-empt parliament's decision on the replacement of Trident", itemising better uses (including conventional forces) for the funding[33]. The issue of whether Britain needs nuclear weapons seems likely to be a lively one in the months to come.

A related cause for Corbyn is the Stop the War

32 Report by Asa Bennett, *The Daily Telegraph* [April 9th 2015]
33 BBC Television News [August 31st 2015]

Campaign, formed in the wake of the 9/11 attacks of 2001 in the US to try to dissuade the Bush administration from going to war in Afghanistan, where (the CIA believed) Osama bin Laden, the perceived mastermind of the attacks, was holed up. When George W Bush launched the so-called War on Terror, he recruited the support of Tony Blair, first in the Afghanistan adventure, then in the unrelated invasion of Iraq (proposed seemingly because Bush believed that the Iraqi ruler Saddam Hussein had tried to arrange the killing of his father, the first President Bush: "This is the guy who tried to kill my Dad"[34]).

SWC dedicated itself to opposing the Iraq War in particular and the general War on Terror. The Iraqi invasion was widely opposed in Britain and, ahead of it, Stop the War led a 'Not in My Name' march through London of as many as two million supporters. Speakers included Tony Benn and Charles Kennedy, the Liberal Democrat leader. No Lib Dem MP supported the invasion of Iraq and many Labour MPs defied three-line whips to vote against the Blair government's developing stance. On February 25th, 121 backbenchers defied the three-line whip. Three weeks later, the number had risen to 140, among them Robin Cook and John Denham, who had resigned from the government,

---

34 Quoted by Jim Lobe on *Common Dreams* website [October 19th 2004]

and other former ministers including Frank Dobson, Chris Smith, Glenda Jackson, Doug Henderson, Gavin Strang, Chris Mullin and Mark Fisher.

Corbyn spoke at another huge rally called at short notice after the invasion began: "I seem to remember being told by Tony Blair and Jack Straw[35] last September and last October that there was no question that Britain would go to war without there being a moral, ethical, legal and United Nations basis for it. Well, Tony, there is no moral basis for bombing Baghdad and Basra, there is no legal authority – you didn't even put a resolution to the UN because you knew that, despite all the bribery and the money that was offered over the past few months, not one country in the world other than Britain and the United States was prepared to vote for war"[36].

Corbyn's continuing approach to the Middle East draws unexpected support from a former chief political commentator of *The Daily Telegraph*, one who perhaps admires the man's plain speaking: "Corbyn is our only current hope of any serious challenge to a failed orthodoxy. Blair and Cameron have both adopted a foreign policy based on subservience rather than partnership with the

35 Then Foreign Secretary
36 Stop the War Rally: Innovative Minds website [March 22nd 2003]

United States, which has done grave damage to British interests.

"In the Middle East this approach has ensured that we are confronting a growing terrorist threat in the region with an ever-decreasing base in popular support, and actually hated by an ever-growing population who identify Britain with their oppressors. There is no country in the Middle East, or around the world, where Britons are safer, or can do business more securely, as a result of Blairite policy. Mr Corbyn's critics always claim that they want democracy. But do they really? They only want democracy, so long as democracy does not threaten the interests of their powerful backers". This is Peter Oborne[37].

Another global concern draws support for Corbyn's position, again from Paul Rogers: "David Cameron's government is now paying little more than lip service to green issues, and the UK has slipped way behind many other Western governments on renewables and related matters. However, December's climate change summit in Paris and the current surge in global warming both mean that a vigorous party focusing on this issue may attract far more attention, and get more support, than expected"[38].

37 *Middle East Eye* [August 27th 2015]
38 *Op cit*

Another grouping joined was the Anti-Apartheid Movement, on the National Executive of which Corbyn served for some years. When Margaret Thatcher invited South African President PW Botha to London in June 1984, a week-long picket of South Africa House in Trafalgar Square was planned. The Metropolitan Police attempted to impose and enforce a ban on demonstrations within the vicinity of the Square. Waves of protesters defied the ban and were detained by the police, among them Corbyn and fellow MPs Stuart Holland and Tony Banks. The legality of the ban was successfully challenged and all charges promptly dropped. A news shot of Corbyn being led away by police has been widely circulated.

Further causes taken up in his first decade as an MP were the miscarriages of justice – as both turned out to be – imposed on the men and women known respectively as the Guildford Four and the Birmingham Six. The first group, along with associates known as the Maguire Seven, all confessed to planting bombs at two pubs in Guildford in October 1974, causing 70 casualties, five of them fatal. The second group, who did not all confess, were accused of planting two bombs in Birmingham pubs the following month; 21 were killed and 182 injured. Both groups alleged intimidation, torture, beatings, sleep and food deprivation and threats to their families while in custody. All were convicted, but after a long series of appeals and retrials all were exonerated and finally compensated. One of the Maguire Seven died while still in prison.

Reminiscing in an interview in the *Islington Tribune* to mark reaching thirty years in parliament, Corbyn cited as the high point of his time: "The release of the Birmingham Six in 1991 and the Guildford Four in 1989 was amazing. I had helped campaign for them because of a miscarriage of justice and I could paper the walls with abusive letters I got at the time"[39].

Another Corbyn cause – perhaps the one bringing more contumely on his head than any other – is that of Palestine. Corbyn is a patron of the Palestine Solidarity Campaign, founded the year before he became an MP, and he supports its policy of boycotting Israeli exports. There are no issues more incendiary than those of Israel and its neighbours, of Zionism and caliphatism, of anti-Semitism and Islamophobia. The blandest or most objective comment on any of these matters is attacked in the fiercest terms. Nothing I write here will escape censure from some quarter.

Here is a measure of the kind of coverage that

---

39 June 7th 2013

Corbyn receives: "Left-wing extremist ... half-educated fanatic ... A dogmatic socialist who was quick to appoint a supporter of Castroite Cuba[40] as his spokesman on the economy, Corbyn has backed the 'titanic struggle' of the Ba'athist and Islamist mass murderers responsible for the slaughter of scores of thousands of civilians, as well as thousands of American and British troops, in post-Saddam Iraq. He is an apologist for the dictatorship of the ayatollahs in Iran ...

"He is a longstanding associate of the anti-Semitic organisation Deir Yassin Remembered, which is run by Holocaust deniers. He described the genocidal criminals of Hamas and Hezbollah as 'friends'. He championed the Islamist cleric Raed Salah, a proponent of blood libels". This closely argued analysis is by Paul Bogdanor in *The Algemeiner Journal*, published in New York[41]. The only identified bases for any of his assertions are "a well-placed source in his campaign team" (oh, we can all contrive one of those) and some unnamed demonstrators at the September visit of Israeli Prime Minister Benjamin Netanyahu to London.

---

40 Well-known extremist Pope Francis met Fidel Castro in Cuba in September 2015

41 'Jeremy Corbyn Is Placing Himself at the Head of Britain's "Palestine Solidarity" Lynch Mobs' [September 17th 2015]

So is there merit in these horrendous charges? I don't propose to address the *ad hominem* ingredients – readers may make their own assessments. John McDonnell (now shadow Chancellor) is indeed a long-standing supporter of Cuba; there has been no version of Cuba save a "Castroite" one these 55 years. To pick out this cause seems perverse, mere months after Washington's détente with Havana, of which Barack Obama said: "The best way to support our values is through engagement"[42], chiming exactly with Corbyn's own global strategy. The point about Iran too had already been overtaken by events when Bogdanor made it.

The phrase "titanic struggle" derives from a statement issued by the Stop the War Coalition (then so-called) in the light of the occupation of Iraq by American and British troops the previous month: "The Iraqis themselves are now engaged in a titanic struggle to rid their country of occupying forces"[43]. To the millions believing the invasion to have been unjustifiable, and questionable at best in international law, the sentiment seems unexceptionable.

Now I come to the allegations that are used to blackguard Corbyn's reputation regarding Jews.

---

42 July 1st 2015
43 June 25th 2003

The story of Deir Yassin is too substantial to rehearse here – it may be easily accessed on-line – but in short it concerns an Arab village of that name where dozens of civilians were massacred by paramilitaries in 1948. The village was repopulated by Jewish settlers. The bare facts are not in dispute: the Israeli Prime Minister David Ben-Gurion formally apologised to King Abdullah of Transjordan.

The question of whether Deir Yassin Remembered is "run by Holocaust deniers" is presented disingenuously and misleadingly. It is based on a dubious report in the *Daily Mail*[44] that Corbyn has "long-standing links" with a "notorious" Holocaust denier called Paul Eisen. Far from being notorious, Eisen (who is Jewish) was wholly obscure until Internet trawlers at the Rothermere paper turned up his nine week-old blog (which is open to invited readers only, perhaps as a result of his rise to 'notoriety') and parlayed his self-important vapourings into their version of cast-iron fact. Conveniently for conspiracy-inventors, Eisen is a constituent of Corbyn's, which means that he has met the MP, as have tens of thousands of other North Islington residents. It is plainly a defect of democracy that an MP cannot pick his voters.

---

44 August 7th 2015

Insofar as tracing Eisen's idiosyncratic views is possible, the description "Holocaust denier" (though his own) is rather wide of the mark. He is no David Irving. What he seems to do is to part company with some details of the orthodox Shoah narrative. There seems some evidence that Eisen acted as what can only be dubbed an 'entryist' into both Deir Yassin Remembered and the Palestine Solidarity Campaign. The aspect informing his interest in the former was his discovery that Yad Vashem, the Holocaust Museum, is built very close to the site of Deir Yassin.

Among letters supporting Corbyn on the matter, this was unusually telling: "Corbyn has promoted negotiations between Israel and Hamas which have also been advocated for almost a decade now by Efraim Halevy, the former head of Mossad, and Shlomo Gazit, the former head of Israel's Shin Bet intelligence agency. While Corbyn promotes peace, many of his critics promote sales. Gordon Brown's government armed Israel throughout the 2008-09 Gaza war in which Amnesty and other human rights groups found evidence strongly suggesting Israeli forces targeted civilians. The current government has lifted the last restrictions on arms sales to Israel despite Amnesty international reporting war crimes against civilians in Netanyahu's last Gaza war. If Corbyn was Prime Minister he would not be arming Israel or Hamas"[45].

As to Hamas and Hezbollah being his 'friends', I shall separate these out. Hamas forms the democratically elected government of Palestine. It is deemed a terrorist organisation by the US, the EU and a small number of countries including Egypt and, of course, Israel, but only its military wing is prescribed by Britain. Hezbollah, which is based in Lebanon, was born out of resistance to the Israeli invasion of Lebanon in 1982; neither Britain nor the US lists its non-military manifestation as 'terrorist'. The UN designates no part of Hamas or Hezbollah 'terrorist'.

In the 1940s, there was an organisation linked to violent acts that would now be termed terrorism by many. It was called Irgun and it played its part in the Deir Yassin massacre and was allegedly responsible for the 1946 bombing of the King David Hotel in Jerusalem, which killed 91 people, Jewish, British and Arab. The head of Irgun, Menachem Begin, went on to serve as Israeli Prime Minister, the first leader of a government formed by the Likud party. Begin took part in the Camp David Accords with Egypt's Anwar Sadat, brokered by Jimmy Carter, and he and Sadat were awarded the Nobel Peace Prize. Had no one agreed to be 'friends' with

---

45 Duncan McFarlane, letters to *The Guardian* [August 20th 2015]

Begin, the course of Middle East history would have been very different.

There is nothing to Corbyn referring to these terrorist/not terrorist organisations as 'friends'. It's the term Corbyn always uses when meeting people, whether literally true or merely amicable. If he used the word 'comrades' or the term 'brothers and sisters', he would be attacked for that instead. More seriously, if no more appropriately, he is often accused of 'only' meeting terrorists and other undesirables. It's a pity that his meetings with the Beard Liberation Front (yes, it does exist) go unremarked. "Why doesn't he meet any right-wingers?" his critics demand, assuming their question is unanswerable.

Think about it. Progress towards peace requires what Churchill called "jaw-jaw rather than war-war". Jaw-jaw requires both sides to attend and talk. Had Corbyn invited Netanyahu to meet him on the latter's London visit, do you suppose the Israeli premier would have accepted? When Augusto Pinochet was held under British house arrest for a year and a half at the end of the 1990s, do you imagine that his chief apologist, Margaret Thatcher, would have been only too happy to arrange tea with the General for Corbyn?

Finally, there is Raed Salah. He is a 57-year-old Israeli-born Arab who has served three times as mayor in the predominantly Arab city of Umm al-Fahm in the Haifa District. As may be imagined, he is a fierce critic of Israeli government policy and a frequent target of official harassment, including imprisonment on charges the merit of which he disputes. In 2011, Salah travelled to Britain to meet Palestine Solidarity Campaign officials (including Corbyn) but was pre-empted by being arrested and detained. An English court overturned the detention and awarded him damages.

In 2008, Salah was charged with incitement to violence and racism in a speech he had given in Jerusalem a year before (the delay is not explained). He was quoted thus: "We have never allowed ourselves to knead [the dough for] the bread that breaks the fast in the holy month of Ramadan with children's blood. Whoever wants a more thorough explanation, let him ask what used to happen to some children in Europe, whose blood was mixed in with the dough of the [Jewish] holy bread"[46]. The word Jewish, inserted by the reporter, was not used by Salah, who was acquitted of the racism charge. In *The Guardian* later, Salah explicitly repudiated any use of the 'blood libel' but the passage was edited out[47].

---

46 Report in *Haaretz* [January 29th 2008]
47 April 19th 2012

The words of which he was accused are a variation on the so-called 'blood libel' (*pace* Bogdanor, there is only the one) which proposes that, during the Middle Ages, Jews murdered Christian children and ritually added their blood to matzah during Pesach. The nature of the calumny is obviously repugnant, but sadly offensive imagery is not uncommon across the Middle East political spectrum.

During Operation Protective Edge, the seven weeks of bombardment of Gaza by Israel in 2014, a friend who has family in Israel, someone with an Oxbridge degree whose career has been spent in the media, informed me gravely that Palestinian mothers place their babies on the roofs of their houses so that they are more likely to be killed and be added to the child casualty figures. It seemed extraordinary that someone with that history and knowledge could fail to recognise black propaganda.

Bogdanor omitted what you might have expected him to see as his bogeyman's responsibility for thousands of murders in the UK. Corbyn is often characterised as an apologist for the IRA, which would be comedy if it were not meant damagingly. In a wide-ranging interview about international issues, he spoke on Ireland: "The relationship between Britain and Ireland has been fundamentally an abusive one ... During the 1980s ... we built up regular contacts with Sinn Féin. We were condemned by our own party leadership for so doing ... and we were proved right. In the end, even Margaret Thatcher recognised that there had to be some kind of political settlement in Ireland, that militarily it wasn't going to be possible, and eventually this became the Good Friday Agreement after the 1997 election ... a very important staging post ... Ultimately, I think Ireland has to be united and I think Ireland will be united. In fact it's already happening. In reality, health policy, transport policy, environment policy, so many things are jointly determined between the north and the south" and he drew a parallel with Palestine[48].

Particular scorn has been reserved for Corbyn's long-time ally, John McDonnell. At a London gathering in 2003 to commemorate the IRA hunger strikers of 1981 (an annual event at which he had spoken for more than ten years), he said: "It's about time we started honouring those people involved in the armed struggle. It was the bombs and bullets and sacrifice made by the likes of Bobby Sands that brought Britain to the negotiating table. The peace we have now is due to the action of the IRA"[49].

48 *The VIP Show*, interview with Hassan Alkatib on the Aletejah Channel [July 25th 2015]

49 Quoted, BBC News website [May 30th 2003]

Sands had been sentenced to fourteen years in the Maze prison for possession of handguns. There is no evidence that he ever killed anyone, but at sixteen he had been held at gunpoint by Protestant gang members outside his place of work and his family were twice forced to move by neighbourhood gangs. It would be idle to pretend that there was not substantial support for the hunger strikers in Northern Ireland and beyond. While in jail, Sands won a parliamentary seat at a by-election in Fermanagh and Tyrone, as the result of which the Thatcher government changed the law in order to prevent serving prisoners being nominated for election.

No record seems to have survived of McDonnell's other remarks at the Sands event that might have provided context. But three days later, he wrote an article which addressed the controversy that had then been sparked: "The next breakthrough in the peace process needs to offer the prospect of a lasting solution, but this will only come with a dramatic change in how we confront the trauma experienced over Northern Ireland. On all sides we have to start telling each other some hard truths ... I abhor the killing of innocent human beings. My argument was that republicans had the right to honour those who had brought about [the] process of negotiation which had led to peace ...

"I see my task now as doing all I can to get the political show back on the road, to create the kinds of formulations through which the IRA, the loyalist paramilitaries and the British army can depart the scene without a sense of abiding grievance. No side will move if movement is portrayed as humiliating surrender ...

"Irish republicans have to face the fact that the use of violence has resulted in unforgivable atrocities. No cause is worth the loss of a child's life. No amount of political theory will justify what has been perpetrated on the victims of the bombing campaigns. An acknowledgment is also needed that loyalist paramilitaries were motivated by the same dedication to their cause as IRA volunteers and that many British troops demonstrated similar bravery in what was in reality a long and brutal war. Above all else, republicans need to accept that the time for violence has gone. Only the political process offers the real prospect of a united Ireland at peace with itself"[50]. And why did McDonnell consider that he had "a task" in the matter of Irish politics? He was chair of the Labour Party Irish Society and secretary of the all-party parliamentary group Irish in Britain.

---

50 *The Guardian* [June 3rd 2003]

That McDonnell spoke of "honouring" members of the IRA was dredged up right on cue as soon as Corbyn made him shadow Chancellor. The Tory case against him was primarily an economic one, for McDonnell is as anti-austerity as Corbyn. However, as Chair of Finance for the GLC in the 1980s, McDonnell never ran a deficit and always balanced the books, not a feat that the Tory Chancellor George Osborne has ever achieved.

Challenged on television over his IRA remarks, McDonnell offered this: "I accept it was a mistake to use those words, but actually if it contributed towards saving one life, or preventing someone else being maimed it was worth doing, because we did hold on to the peace process. There was a real risk of the republican movement splitting and some of them continuing the armed process. If I gave offence, and I clearly have, from the bottom of my heart I apologise, I apologise"[51].

I'm not a fan of political apologies. They smack of gesture politics, certainly when they cost the apologist nothing. David Cameron was given credit for apologising to the people of Northern Ireland for the Bloody Sunday massacre, but he was five at the time it occurred. He might as well have said sorry for the potato famine.

---

51 *Question Time* BBC1 [September 17th 2015]

On the other hand, regret stuck in his craw when, ahead of his first official visit to Jamaica, he was called upon to recognise Britain's role in the lamentable history of slavery. The chairman of the Caricom Reparations Commission, Sir Hilary Beckles, wrote an open letter to Cameron, noting that "You are a grandson of the Jamaican soil who has been privileged and enriched by your forbears' sins of the enslavement of our ancestors ... We ask not for handouts or any such acts of indecent submission. We merely ask that you acknowledge responsibility for your share of this situation and move to contribute in a joint programme of rehabilitation and renewal".

Downing Street's response to this dignified and restrained approach was to declare that "we don't think reparations is the right approach. The PM's point will be he wants to focus on the future. We are talking about issues that are centuries old and taken under a different government when he was not even born"[52]. In other words, apologies are made only when they suit the apologist.

The media soothsayers assured us that Corbyn would be putting clear water between himself and the Blairite past by apologising for the Iraq invasion in his address to the Party Conference. No one seemed to remark that the apology never came.

---

52 Report, *The Guardian* [September 29th 2015]

Perhaps Corbyn too does not care for gesture politics.

Where tangible recompense is proper it should be made. Otherwise, being sorry butters no parsnips. But if you're going to do it, you have to do it unconditionally. Many scoffed at McDonnell because he qualified his apology with "if I gave offence", but in fact (as the reader may see) he 'withdrew' that qualification. It would have been best had he simply said "from the bottom of my heart, I apologise"; that formulation (even if hung about) ought to be sufficient for any fair-minded person.

I can promise you that Andy Burnham, Yvette Cooper, Liz Kendall and George Osborne, Boris Johnson, Theresa May, Tim Farron and all the other would-be Prime Ministers made loose remarks in their respective youths[53] that they wouldn't want to make under the spotlight of public life. The best they could hope to do about such remarks would be to apologise humbly and move on.

Any connection that can be made between the left and terrorism is grist to the Tory press. What's more, some editors have no compunction about the accuracy of the report or even whether

_____

53 Indeed we are now told that David Cameron (henceforth known – Boccaccio includes bestiality in his compendium – as 'The Decameron') indulged some unseemly behaviour, not least inserting his penis in the mouth of a dead pig while stoned at a party

it has already been withdrawn. A Murdoch paper happily went with the following: "Jeremy Corbyn tried to fund an IRA bomber's flight from British cops when he was caught by a clever fraudster, *The Sun* can reveal. The embattled new Labour leader handed over £45 to Irishman Sean O'Regan, who approached him inside Parliament to claim he was part of an IRA active service unit. Having pulled off the trick, which extraordinarily also included the claim to Mr Corbyn that he had planted bombs in London and now needed to escape, the conman was later caught and convicted of fraud for it.

"Revelation of the bizarre incident that erupted in 1987 – at the height of the bloody Troubles – left MPs on all sides of the Commons staggered last night. It renews serious concerns over Mr Corbyn's judgment and whether he can be trusted with national security secrets. Conservative MP Conor Burns questions whether 'sensitive information' should now be shared with the Leader of the Opposition: 'If Corbyn could give cash to someone he thought was an IRA terrorist, could he easily give secrets to our enemies within or without?'[54]".

On the face of it, the story raises a grave concern. But what is "extraordinary" and "bizarre" and leaves the reader "staggered" is that *The Sun* does not appear to have access to the files of its

54 *The Sun* [September 19th 2015]

sister paper, *The Times*, wherein this appeared at the time of the "incident": "In an agency report 'MP was duped' (January 31) we said that Jeremy Corbyn, MP for Islington North, was approached in the House of Commons by a confidence trickster posing as an IRA bomber and that he gave him £45. We have been asked to make it clear that it was not Mr Corbyn but a member of his staff in his constituency office who paid the confidence trickster the money. When Mr Corbyn found out about the incident he immediately notified the police. We apologise for this error"[55]. I can find no evidence of an apology from Conor Burns or *The Sun*.

The constant refrain – that Corbyn consorts with people who mean you harm – is intended to do him a lot more harm than he might do you. The fact that politicians of all stripes constantly meet (either openly or clandestinely) people you wouldn't want in your home is of no consequence when the urgent work of undermining Corbyn's appeal is the goal.

His motives in being accessible are always questioned and frequently belittled: "When the anointed one is the incarnation of principle, his actions are beyond reproach. Scrutiny of his opinions and the company he has kept are 'smears'. If he has invited to parliament men who

---

55 *The Times* [February 17th 1987]

justify terrorism or shared platforms with anti-Semites and homophobes, it cannot be because his judgment is warped. It must be an enlightened strategy of engagement for the higher cause of peace"[56].

In late 2015 George Osborne was in China making deals with a Communist government whose record on human rights is about as lamentable as any on the planet. The clue that this is perfectly acceptable is in the phrase "making deals". That Osborne holds his nose (if indeed he does) and meets leaders who may easily be pilloried as monsters is fine because it is "in the British interest". All sorts of dubious deals are morally cleansed by the quest for self-interest. Patriotism – if that is what I am describing – trumps any moral scruple.

Self-interest has a fundamental appeal for Conservatism. In the European elections of 2004, Michael Howard's Tories were even permitted to be designated on the actual ballot paper as "The Conservative Party – Putting Britain First", though what that meant in practice was never explained; but surely being *communautaire* suggests putting *Europe* first.

I may be naïve, but I have always subscribed to a sentiment that, of all people, the aforementioned

56 Rafael Behr, *The Guardian* [September 2nd 2015]

Osborne famously articulated: "we are all in this together"[57]. Evidently though, Osborne was not referring to the global population when he said 'all'; well, I am. For unless policies are developed that benefit every part of the planet – and I am thinking not only of climate change, though that is of course of primary concern – the problems of the planet will only worsen. My sense of Corbyn's philosophy is that, as I would, he would identify himself first not as an Englishman but as a citizen of the world. It is only by adopting a global view that one can usefully and truly represent the British interest.

Yet still it goes on: "If you judge a man by the company he keeps — and that is generally a fair way of looking at our fellow human beings — Jeremy Corbyn has associated with some very unpleasant people since becoming an MP more than 30 years ago" writes the UKIP admirer Stephen Glover[58].

As for David Cameron's unpleasant people, two words will suffice: Saudi Arabia. Here is Cameron rationalising his decision to lower to half-mast union flags on government buildings at the death of the Saudi King Abdullah: "You have to build strong relationships sometimes with regimes that you don't always agree with. That I think is part of

57 Speech to the Tory Party Conference, reported on the BBC News website [October 6th 2009]
58 Daily Mail [August 20th 2015]

the job"[59]. What's sauce for that goose is sauce for Labour's gander.

As a gay man, I have been challenged more than once to defend Corbyn's willingness to meet people who believe that homosexuality is a mortal sin and even a capital offence. I have no difficulty in defending it because Corbyn's motive is always to build bridges. In any case, he has nothing to defend in his support of gay rights. Immediately upon becoming an MP in 1983, he spoke on a 'No Socialism without Gay Liberation' platform[60]. He has "consistently voted for equal gay rights"[61]. In a mathematical analysis of his voting record on LGBT rights, Corbyn scores 95.3 per cent[62]. That's good enough for me.

As in other things, other politicians are not judged by the lofty standards that are imposed on Corbyn. That paragon of virtue the Tony Blair Faith Foundation is part-funded by the Junk Bond King Michael Milken, who has served time and been fined millions of dollars for "the biggest fraud case in the history of the securities industry"[63], and his racketeering-indicted brother Lowell.

Tony Blair's followers characterise Corbyn as a throwback to the politics of the 1970s and '80s.

59 Sky News interview [February 2nd 2015]
60 BBC News website [September 12th 2015]
61 *TheyWorkForYou* website
62 *The Public Whip* website
63 *The New York Times* [April 26th 1990]

How little they know. His roots lie much deeper – in the Diggers, John Lilburne and the Levellers, Tom Paine, the Owenites, William Cobbett, the Chartists, Blake and Coleridge and Burns, John Bright, Edward Carpenter and Robert Tressell. This is a living tradition. The Blairites, on the other hand, represent a fashion whose time is gone.

With uncharacteristic even-handedness, *The Daily Telegraph* let one of its more progressive journalists – in fact there are several on the paper and always were – write against editorial orthodoxy: "I have a vote in the Labour leadership election, and I'm giving it to Jeremy Corbyn ... The leader we Labour members choose will fundamentally affect how we organise, what we prioritise – the whole direction of the movement during the next five years. And you know what? Blair and [Alastair] Campbell are not going to spend those five years meeting in slightly shoddy municipal buildings or cold church halls, trying to decide how to keep that movement alive and connect with the electorate while we're out of power. People like me are. So they can have all the opinions they want, but they'll have to excuse us for not giving two hoots – it's an obvious point but worth saying that the Labour party's future ultimately belongs in the hands of its actual members, not Establishment commentators"[64].

64 Helen Coffey [August 17th 2015]. Her piece gathered 2.5 million 'likes' on the paper's website, compared to 269 for an editorial headed 'Jeremy Corbyn must be stopped' five days later

After Labour lost the 1970 election, the BBC transmitted a frankly scurrilous programme, called *Yesterday's Men*, which purported to examine the leadership's first year in opposition but tricked the participants into compromise and ridicule[65]. Harold Wilson was incandescent with rage, especially when a subsequent companion programme, *Mr Heath's Quiet Revolution*, gave the government a gently easy ride. Anthony Smith (then editor of the hosting slot, *24 Hours*, now the retired President of Magdalen, Oxford) called it "the biggest and most furious row that a television programme in the English language has ever provoked"[66].

Wilson and his ministers turned out to be tomorrow's men – they formed another government less than three years after the BBC's affront – and Wilson never forgave the Corporation; perhaps his subsequent lamentable appearances as a BBC chat host were a perverse sort of revenge. But Blair and his allies are not coming back; they *are* yesterday's men.

Famously, Corbyn has defied the party whip frequently. The Public Whip website, a source for voting records, goes back only to 1997 and, since then, logs 533 votes when he "rebelled" (by which

65 Presented by David Dimbleby, produced by Angela Pope BBC1 [June 16th 1971]
66 Quoted in *Television Policies of the Labour Party 1951-2001* by Des Freedman [Routledge 2003]

the site "means a vote against the majority vote by members of the MP's party"). Among the issues on which he voted against the party leadership were ID cards, increased tuition fees and the invasion of Iraq.

However, Corbyn has never been sent into purdah by having the whip removed, which means in practice that the member has to sit as an independent for the duration of the punishment with all the benefits of party membership withdrawn. Indeed, in the Labour Party at least, the whip is almost never withdrawn for 'rebellion' but for malpractice (Jack Straw and the Tory Sir Malcolm Rifkind, both former foreign secretaries, lost the whip in 2015 while their probity or otherwise was examined by the parliamentary standards committee; it was then restored). What persistent rebellion brings is being overlooked for party preferment, an exclusion that Corbyn has now triumphantly confounded by democratic acclaim.

CHAPTER 2: UNELECTABLE

Two issues raged in the Labour Party over Corbyn's inexorable rise. The notion that he was 'unelectable', not so much by party members as by the wider electorate, was both held sincerely by many and used cynically by his rivals. Liz Kendall, the most Blairite leadership candidate and so positioned the furthest from Corbyn, reckoned in *The Observer* that his young supporters were not old enough to recall Labour losing "election after election in the 1980s"[67]. This was characteristic of the way history was used selectively against Corbyn. After Michael Foot was elected Labour leader in 1980, the party fractured and several former ministers left to form a new centrist party, the Social Democratic Party (SDP). Partly in consequence, Labour was defeated in the election of 1983[68]. Kendall was ten years of age at the time of the party split, so it may be doubted that her memory of the sequence of events is keenly informed or analytical.

---

67 August 2nd 2015

68 Incidentally, at that election, Corbyn entered the Commons for the first time, winning his Islington North seat with a remarkable 26 per cent increase on his predecessor's majority, despite a 9.3 per cent decline in Labour's vote nationally. From the get-go, he has always managed to command significant personal popularity that translates into votes

By contrast, I am old enough to recall the horror felt by followers of the late Labour leader Hugh Gaitskell when Harold Wilson became his successor in 1963 (I was 15). Wilson was an old ally of Nye Bevan, Gaitskell's great rival on the party's left. The Gaitskellites were right-wingers. However, the former leader, Clement Attlee, did not gratuitously intervene (as former leader Blair did three times in the 2015 leader election) and the right-wingers did not defect. Wilson held the party together pretty effectively and won four general elections, one more than Tony Blair and without seeing his majority dwindle successively as Blair did.

Comparisons with Foot ignore some salient factors. He was voted leader by a ballot of MPs, the poll confined to their number. No popular *soulèvement* sustained him, nor was there any precipitous rise in party membership as has been inspired by Corbyn. Foot had a narrow win over his more right-wing rival Denis Healey, who died in October 2015; Healey was so sure of victory that he refused to countenance any other result – I recall his smug face doing so in a television interview.

But Healey's brusque and cavalier manner alienated some MPs and there was growing support for the more radical Tony Benn in the party

(Healey subsequently held off a challenge by Benn for the post of deputy leader by less than one per cent of the vote).

Great man though he was, Foot was never likely to connect with the wider public. He wasn't averse to the 180-degree turn. Just a fortnight after accounting himself "an inveterate peacemonger" in the House, he committed his party to supporting the government in going to war with Argentina over the Falkland Islands. It seems most unlikely that Corbyn will ever perform a somersault like that. Had Labour opposed or abstained in the vote, the public support for the Falklands venture might have been rather more tepid. As it turned out, the war and its winning turned Margaret Thatcher from the unpopular, insular leader of a fading power to a colossus on the global stage. That was a significant factor in her beating Foot's Labour Party so decisively in the 1983 general election.

Foot seemed remote and professorial, more likely to be diverted by books (Swift, Paine, Hazlitt) than by the realities of politics. This was to misunderstand him, of course. He was an adherent as well as a biographer of Aneurin Bevan, succeeding to Bevan's old parliamentary seat of Ebbw Vale after his mentor's death.

For his part, Jeremy Corbyn is a voracious and informed reader. In his address to the Party

Conference, he quoted Maya Angelou and Ben Okri, which must have delighted discriminating readers in his audience. These are rather more encouraging cultural markers than David Cameron produces – Michael Winner in a television commercial, for instance, or listening to Supertramp. Rather than as an academic, Corbyn comes across like a schoolmaster or local GP, the kind everyone has encountered and come to trust. That plays much stronger than Foot's more eccentric, dramatic manner.

It is argued (by people who find such things of interest) that Corbyn's attachment to the beard he has worn all his adult life is a 'turn-off'. Evidently he is the first unshaven leader of any British party since Labour's first, Keir Hardie. That may be. Nonetheless, Tony Blair's first cabinet in 1997 numbered four bearded Secretaries of State: Robin Cook, Alastair Darling, David Blunkett and Frank Dobson. The Palace of Westminster roof did not fall in.

One may argue that a leader from the left of the party is as electable as one from the right – or what is considered the centre ground of British politics, the Tories being to the right. David Cameron is generally thought of as a 'centre-right' politician, as Tony Blair, in his days as Labour leader and Prime Minister, was deemed 'centre-left'.

There is a consensus between mainstream politicians and the press that the centre ground is where serious politicians pitch camp and from whence they supposedly win elections. Of course that has been true on occasion but it discounts changes in public sentiment. And it is another highly selective view. That snorting noise you hear comes from the grave of Margaret Thatcher.

Thatcher exemplifies how a game-changing political insurgency was able to confound what economist JK Galbraith dubbed "the conventional wisdom"[69]. After Harold Wilson regained a majority in the second of the two 1974 general elections, Thatcher mounted an unexpected challenge to the defeated Tory leader Edward Heath, who was demonstrating no interest in stepping down. (My mother and I were eating at the late Soho restaurant L'Epicure sometime in 1974 when we noticed Thatcher at the next table, dining *à deux* with a man whom we later were able to identify as Airey Neave, her closest confidant. I wish now that we had eavesdropped more diligently. They must certainly have been plotting).

Virtually no one imagined Thatcher would worst Heath, who had called the leadership election specifically to reconfirm his support as leader. And of course Thatcher was, like Corbyn,

69 *The Affluent Society* [1958]

a kind of insurgent. She represented a much less consensual, much more fundamentalist version of Conservatism. The party's old guard – privately educated landowners downing brandies in their all-male clubs and finding women in politics a somewhat irritating joke – knew in their bones that she was perfectly unelectable. As Thatcher's biographer Charles Moore put it: "Many regarded her candidacy as nothing more than a chance to prepare the ground for challenges by someone more serious, or merely for malcontents to let off steam"[70].

Woodrow Wyatt, a journalist and Labour MP who had lost his seat in 1970, declared in the *Sunday Mirror* that Thatcher would lead the Tories in "an extremist, class-conscious, right-wing direction" which would keep the party out of office for a decade. Does that sound familiar? Wyatt was to become a close ally of Thatcher who knighted him and then raised him to the Lords. In fact, not one newspaper preferred her to Heath.

Charles Moore also recorded that "as the campaign entered its closing phase, the 'establishment' which Mrs Thatcher had decided to take on pulled out all the stops"[71]; *cf.* the 2015 Labour leadership campaign. Yet Thatcher won (as

---

70 *Margaret Thatcher: The Authorized Biography* volume 1 [Allen Lane 2013]
71 *ibid*

Corbyn has done) and she went on to transform the political landscape as Corbyn could. You may argue until Tory-blue in the face that the way a party wins power is by appealing across the middle ground to peel voters from the rival large party, a truism for commentators and practitioners. Thatcher stands in triumphant refutation.

The fairy story with which I began this book will have been dismissed by some readers as impossibly simplistic. I counsel caution. Those who inhabit the Westminster village and who closely follow its affairs bandy around a lot of terms that need no explanation to each other: right-wing, centre ground, left-wing, Thatcherite, Blairite, progressive, reactionary, neoliberal, socialist and so on. They converse in unusually discursive and subtle ways. They know what they mean and their interlocutors do too.

But the great majority of voters don't talk this way. Ask a random voter in the street to define centrist or interventionist or liberal and she may struggle to offer anything very accurate or coherent. Most people listen to their gut instincts when voting: do I trust him? Is she sincere? Are they the sort of people who understand my situation? It may be disheartening for the political wonk to be told that his educated vote is worth no more than that of someone who votes out of some half-conscious crush on the candidate or because the candidate drives the same make of car as the voter or because the voter's parents always voted for this party and, in this constituency, the proverbial donkey would get elected if it had the appropriate party allegiance. But that is how it is.

Political issues are often complex. Politicians try to frame answers to questions that are comprehensive, nuanced and proof against any eventuality, but such answers can appear merely evasive. No wonder they always talk about having to make 'difficult decisions'. Such decisions frequently are indeed difficult, especially if what is uppermost in your mind is how the decision will play with the electorate. The voter may well counter that it's precisely to grapple with difficult decisions that we put people into parliament at all.

Jeremy Corbyn has had a great advantage when set against his rivals. Many of the questions of the day lend themselves to immediately comprehensible answers from his perspective: austerity? Trident missiles?: against them; public ownership of the utilities? redistribution of wealth?: for them. 'End of', as they say. These are not 'difficult' decisions for him. They are logical, rational decisions drawn from his set of principles and values. People who glaze over when politicians weigh in on the benefits of PPI or the dangers of TTIP find Corbyn's clear positions bracing, even when they don't necessarily support them. We like this chap, they say. You know where you stand with him.

Moreover, he does not do politico talk. He eschews phrases like "reaching out" and "going forward" trotted out as if statements of policy as, say, Yvette Cooper is apt to trot out. Perhaps most for this reason, Corbyn has unusual support among that neglected and abused constituency, the young. He has excited hitherto unreachable swathes of the under-25s, a useful future resource when the Labour Party needs to campaign. He has it in him to replicate the momentum of Eugene McCarthy's 'children's crusade' in the 1968 US elections, which might have endured to make a real difference had it not been overtaken by momentous events.

Long after I had made this historical connection, I saw it rubbished by Luke Akehurst in the party publication *Labour List*, though Akehurst misremembered the American phenomenon as occurring at the 1972 election when George McGovern was the Democrat's candidate: "Just as the unworldly idealist McGovern and his hippies were thrashed by the cynical conservatism of Nixon – who proclaimed correctly that he would win because the average American was not young, was not poor and was not black – so Corbyn and his hipster idealists organised by cynical factional hacks would be cruelly destroyed by Lynton Crosby[72] if they are the Labour brand in 2020. McGovern won just Massachusetts and [Washington] DC. Corbyn would do a bit better due to our smaller constituencies, but not a lot – he has pretty much maxed out the market for his type of politics in this internal election, there just isn't a wider set of British voters who want it"[73]. I have two words in reply: Barack Obama.

In any case, who is to say that what has been the case in past elections – or, to be strict, *more often than not* the case in past elections – will always be so in future votes? No two elections are the same. There is no precedent for a nationalist party winning almost 13 per cent of the popular vote as UKIP did at the 2015 general election, nor of a nationalist party (or indeed any kind of party) winning 95 per cent of the seats as the SNP did in Scotland at the same election.

No election replicates the results of a previous one or even the broad pattern of the previous one.

72 David Cameron's election strategist, hired at some expense from Australia
73 July 28th 2015

Despite the consensus branding the 2015 election a 'disaster' for Labour, the party gained seven seats in London, which nobody predicted. What is so noticeable about all these experts – commentators and party *apparatchiks* alike – is how extraordinarily categorical they are about 'what will happen'. They think they know what the voters will do, yet they never learn from past errors.

In media-saturated times, the electorate is less and less likely to perform how it is expected to by psephologists and opinion pollsters. The results of the general elections in 1970, February 1974, 1992 and 2015 confounded the consensus of predictions. Little noticed in the most recent result was the failure to materialise of a supposed advantage for Labour in marginal seats. Analysis of the figures shows that the vote was nothing like as 'catastrophic' for Labour as has been widely claimed, particularly (and conveniently) by those who argue that the party, under Ed Miliband's leadership, moved too far from Blairite orthodoxy.

Although Labour suffered a momentous collapse to the SNP in Scotland – a particular problem that lends itself more readily to constructive address under a Corbyn leadership than any other kind, Corbyn's policies being much closer across a wide range to those of SNP leader

Nicola Sturgeon than those of the other leadership contenders – Labour *increased* its vote in England and Wales by more than a million, comfortably more than the rise in the Conservative vote. Had this increase favoured marginal seats, as had been anticipated, Labour would undoubtedly have gained a majority in the Commons. Instead, the Tories benefited from a concentration of votes gained in the constituencies of their partners in the coalition government of 2010-15, the Liberal Democrats, whose haul of seats dropped from 56 to eight.

If voting figures are unpredictable, political fortunes are more so. Perhaps the most famous remark of the ever-quotable Harold Wilson was: "A week in politics is a long time". It was the truest thing – some would say the only true thing – that Wilson ever said.

My mother died in the summer of 1988. I have always felt that, though she was reasonably well informed about current affairs, she would almost certainly not have heard of the man who became Prime Minister barely thirty months later. John Major's rise from the most obscure post in the cabinet to the top job was truly meteoric, entirely due to events outside his own control. Politics is like that. Zero to hero and back again in the blink of an eye.

Corbyn's transformation from career backbencher, familiar to daily Westminster watchers (if few others) for his perpetual recalcitrance towards the compromises of his own party's leadership, into leader of that party was not something anybody – absolutely anybody at all anywhere in the world – could have anticipated even as recently as the closing of nominations for leadership candidacy, let alone at the start of the 2015 general election campaign. When he decided to run, the bookies made him 200/1.

That Corbyn's majority in his own seat of Islington North rose from 12,401 in 2010 to 21,194 in 2015 did not especially signify. Labour did do well in London. In Streatham, Chuka Umunna's majority similarly rose from 3,259 to 13,934; Umunna, who was briefly a candidate for the Labour leadership after Ed Miliband fell on his sword, was a Liz Kendall supporter and declined to join Corbyn's shadow cabinet. He will be an articulate thorn in Corbyn's flesh.

The new process governing internal party ballots, framed after Ed Miliband's last-gasp election as leader over his older brother David in 2010, retained the rule that a candidate has to be nominated by a minimum of 15 per cent of serving members. Corbyn's allies on the left of the party were determined to get one of their own onto the ballot paper and, by Corbyn's own account, it was 'his turn' – the implication is that running is considered a comradely duty on the left (the least benefit always being the recruitment of more followers) and that it was mere luck that Corbyn was this year's patsy. Neither he nor many if any of his allies can have given him a fighting chance. He was short of the required number of MP backers – 35 – until only a few minutes before nominations closed.

Some MPs were persuaded that it would be good for the campaign if the scope of the debate were widened, so they allowed their names to be added to the nomination paper even though they had no intention of actually voting for Corbyn; former shadow Attorney General Emily Thornberry[74] and Margaret Beckett, former Foreign Secretary and deputy party leader[75], were among those lending their names for this purpose. One of Blair's advisors when he was Prime Minister, John McTernan, went on television to denounce these MPs as "morons". This gives some indication of the heat that Corbyn's success has generated in the party.

---

74 Corbyn's parliamentary neighbour in Islington South
75 Dame Margaret was *pro tem* leader for the two months in 1994 after John Smith's untimely death

The language being deployed is frequently more eloquent about the deployer than the object of its use. For instance, the phrase "lurch to the left" is trotted out endlessly, to ensure that no one is in any doubt that the left is no place for sober people to be. That it is such a loaded cliché diminishes the speaker.

Corbyn regularly repeated his fixed resolve that nothing disobliging towards any other Labour member would pass his lips and he seems to have stuck to that. It does not prevent him roundly and cuttingly and sometimes angrily disputing charges made against his policies, stances and indeed his person. And of course the uncontrollable hordes of supporters felt free to weigh in, often in unforgiveable terms and especially on social media. That is a two-way street, however. A lot of inflated rhetoric has been indulged in this contest. Tony Blair especially has talked in dramatic terms of the party "driving over a cliff", of Corbyn needing to be "rugby-tackled" and of his policies embodying *Alice in Wonderland* logic. Disdain for Blair has grown among the Labour grassroots as he eased into a highly lucrative role as a self-appointed global sage.

It's been striking, though, how often Corbyn's political opponents have observed that they like and respect him and find him always courteous and kindly. Corbyn's friend, Tony Benn, was held in great affection for similar reasons across the political spectrum. Since his death in March 2014, a glow has settled over Benn's legend. His candour and courage and wisdom are now recalled with great affection. Of how many politicians do you hear the phrase 'national treasure' used without irony or apology?

That he was Corbyn's mentor is benefiting both the perception of Benn's foresightedness and Corbyn's reputation. Michael Foot too was greatly liked by ally and opponent alike and so was the daddy of them all, Nye Bevan. This instinct to be gracious, amicable and cordial has been carefully handed down on the parliamentary left[76].

The other issue that raged over Corbyn's triumph was that of so-called 'entryism'. To appreciate this concept, one needs some background on both the election rules and Labour Party history. In all parties, the way one member comes to be leader has varied greatly over the years. Until the election of Edward Heath, Tory leaders had 'emerged' from a series of soundings, meetings and deals; Sir Alec Douglas-Home, Heath's immediate predecessor, was not even an

---

76 Home Secretary Theresa May, when Tory party chairman (her own term) in 2002, dubbed the Tories "the nasty party", a phrase that has stuck

MP when thrust forward as not merely party leader but Prime Minister (for Harold Macmillan had resigned from that office, officially due to 'ill health' though he lived another 23 years) – Sir Alec was in the Lords as the 14th Earl of Home.

In the Labour Party, the contest that introduced an electoral college was that of 1994, which made Blair successor to the abruptly deceased John Smith. In that election, Margaret Beckett, Smith's former deputy, was the first woman ever to run for leader (Corbyn voted for her). The rules gave comparable weight to the votes of Labour MPs, constituency party members and affiliates (mostly consisting of trade unions but counting them as blocks). When Blair stepped down in 2007, Gordon Brown was the only candidate as his successor (and hence Prime Minister), John McDonnell having failed to secure sufficient nominations from MPs. McDonnell acted as Corbyn's leadership campaign manager.

In the 2010 election for Brown's successor following the general election defeat, there were five candidates, John McDonnell having withdrawn to avoid taking MPs' nominations from Diane Abbott. She, like Andy Burnham and Ed Balls, received just the qualifying number of nominations and no more, though (as with Corbyn in 2015) some of her 11th hour nominees would not vote for her but considered the left of the party should be represented in the vote. This tactic will not be employed again for many years, I suggest.

The Alternative Vote system (AV) was deployed at this election as at previous leadership polls and for other party and parliamentary posts[77]. As candidates were eliminated, their second preference votes came into play. In the count, Abbott went out in the first round, with Corbyn's one of only seven votes she received. Burnham dropped out next (Corbyn's second preference vote having gone to Ed Miliband), then Balls. In the decisive fourth round, Ed Miliband overtook his brother David for the first time, with only the affiliates clinching the victory, leaving the winner vulnerable to claims that he was "in the pocket of the unions".

In 2013, the then General Secretary of the party, Lord Collins[78], was required by the party to reconsider the election rules. He recommended keeping AV but replacing the electoral college system that had elected Ed Miliband with a one-member-one-vote scheme that, along with existing

77 A UK-wide national referendum offering AV for public elections was defeated two-to-one in 2011
78 Baron Collins of Highbury (which area falls into Corbyn's Islington North seat) was union official Ray Collins and is one of few openly gay people in public life with such a background. *The Collins Review into Labour Party Reform* was published in February 2014. He is now shadow International Development Minister and a Lords whip

party members, permitted participation by non-members who applied to the party and registered their "support for Labour values".

The National Executive Committee of the party then published electoral guidelines including that "Labour Party members on the national membership system and not lapsed from membership at the date set on the timetable will be eligible to vote. Affiliated Supporters and Registered Supporters, as previously defined by the NEC, who have been registered with the Labour Party at the date set on the timetable will be eligible to vote"[79]. Supporters so registering would be required to pay a minimum of £3.

That this would prove in many ways disingenuous was evidently not appreciated at the time. The admittance of 'supporters' of course depended on the sincerity and good faith of those applying. What had not been anticipated was a rush to join the party. In the three months after the general election of 2015, the numbers eligible to vote tripled from a party membership of around 200,000 in May to some 610,000 when registration to vote closed on August 12th, a month before the leadership ballot.

The main motor of this swelling of the electorate was clearly the impact of Corbyn's candidacy.

---

79 *Leadership 2015. Your Choice. Shape the Future* [May 15th 2015]

Three distinct strands were credibly detected in the response, embodying three – in Coleridge's phrase – "contrariant factions"[80]. One consisted of malicious Tories and other opponents of Labour, believing or affecting to believe the notion that a Corbyn-led Labour Party would be 'unelectable'. This cynical ruse was canvassed in print by *The Daily Telegraph*[81], and a junior minister from the coalition government, Tim Loughton, duly sent in his £3 fee. The Labour Party thanked him cordially for his donation but informed him that he would not receive a ballot paper.

Another interest seeking to influence the result was that of groups hostile to Blairism from the non-parliamentary left, which perceived that a leader like Corbyn might act as a 'red wedge' in the party. Some public figures had their votes nullified on this basis, including director Ken Loach, comedians Mark Steel and Jeremy Hardy and union leader Mark Serwotka. But the largest group of new recruits consisted of people who for various reasons had never joined the party (though inclined to support its aims) or who had left the party because of its perceived rightward drift or who found Corbyn a more inspiring political figure than any other in recent memory.

80 *Conciones ad Populum* [1795]
81 *How you can help Corbyn win – and destroy the Labour Party* Unsigned [July 15th 2015]

Labour charged various members of its office staff to seek to distinguish between these factions, a difficult task when the overlap between the second and third groups was so difficult to measure and where a lack of hard evidence meant that cultured guesses had to be taken at applicants' motives. Inevitably, cases of exclusion were trumpeted on social media and readily seen as unjust, particularly as everyone knew that the disputed ballots must, with vanishingly few exceptions, be cast for Corbyn.

Many stories were related that reflected badly on the party and its method of weeding out supposed entryists. One can only take them at face value, being unable to verify them. Here is one such: "My mother-in-law ... who has reached the ripe old age of 90 due to the hundreds of miles she has walked delivering leaflets for the Labour Party, has just been informed she has been barred from voting. [She] joined the Labour Party in the 1940s and spent the next fifty years until she was in her eighties working night and day for the Labour Party.

"The local MP, who did not live in the constituency, stayed at her house when not in London and she was the mainstay in her local ward ... She left the Labour Party in recent years but never joined any other party"[82]. The election

82 Facebook posting, seen as a repost [August 26th 2015]

guidance document also stated: "Any disputes as to the eligibility of and [*sic*[83]] individual members must be raised by the date set on the timetable. The NEC have designated the Director of Governance[84] to rule on eligibility of individual members and her decision will be final"[85].

The verification process continued until polling closed and it was clear that exclusions, both of applications for a vote and of votes already cast, ran into several thousands, though the number was bitterly disputed. Corbyn supporters naturally suspected that a conspiracy was under way to deny the leadership to their man; consequently, given that most predictions gave Corbyn a comfortable lead, probably enough to win on the first ballot[86], his supporters were primed to 'know' that there had been a fix if Yvette Cooper or Andy Burnham won.

According to notes of a meeting of the Labour Party Procedures Committee[87] leaked to *The Guardian*, the party hierarchy was much more exercised by a concern that one of the unsuccessful candidates for the leadership might launch a legal

---

83 Presumably 'any' was meant
84 Her name is Emilie Oldknow
85 *Op cit*
86 As he was most unlikely to be a second preference on a significant number of ballot papers, it was thought essential by his team that he win outright on the first count
87 This was set up for the duration of the election. Acting leader Harriet Harman, party General Secretary Iain McNicol and Margaret Beckett were among its members

challenge on the basis that checks being carried out on applicants to vote were insufficient or discriminatory – a challenge that might come from Burnham or Cooper or Corbyn if the result were sufficiently close – rather than writs being issued by individuals who considered themselves unfairly and perhaps libellously excluded. Legal advice had recommended that the party allow excluded voters to argue their case before any final decision, but a tied vote on the matter meant that the advice was not taken[88]. Nothing came of all this, however. Harriet Harman, the acting leader, continued to describe the process as "robust" to anyone who challenged her.

That the party had imposed upon itself a major headache was clear to everyone. To the supporters of Corbyn, the circle that Harman could not square was the reconciliation of the party's fastidiousness about intruders to its history of eager recruitment. They all remembered the glee with which the party hierarchy welcomed defectors from the woebegone Conservative Party during its years opposing the ministries of Blair and Brown. Alan Howarth, Peter Temple-Morris, Shaun Woodward, Robert Jackson and Quentin Davies had all served in

---

88 August 19th 2015

Tory governments and all "crossed the floor"[89] to Labour and sat for varying periods without seeking confirmation from their electorates. Labour had never before managed to entice sitting Tories onto its benches. All of them tempted the suspicion that their liking for ministerial perks exceeded their party loyalty. Woodward was particularly distrusted – these floor-crossers were comparatively wealthy men but his trappings were conspicuous: he was the only Labour member known to employ a butler. Jeremy Corbyn and Tony Benn were among those demanding that he immediately stand for re-election.

Party loyalty is not a priority for all politicians. Many relish the life of a member of parliament, irrespective of which benches they sit on, and many decide to try for a political career before they decide to which party they might apply. A colleague once told me that his father had been at Oxford with Richard Crossman, who was in Harold Wilson's Cabinet and whose lasting legacy is his three-volume diaries, which set the benchmark for political memoirs. By the father's account, the

89 This is House of Commons jargon for changing parties, a literal crossing of the floor as government and opposition sit facing each other. Sir Hartley Shawcross, the UK's chief prosecutor at the Nuremberg trials of German leaders after World War II, was a Labour minister up until 1951 but was widely expected to change to the Tory side (he never did, though he later sat in the Lords as a so-called cross-bencher with no party allegiance) and hence became known as Sir Shortly Floorcross. Tony Benn's father William crossed the floor from the Liberals to Labour in 1928

student Crossman determined that politics were for him and fixed upon which party to join by the toss of a coin. I believe it.

It's the very purpose of political campaigning that a party wants to gain votes and many – perhaps most – of the votes thus gained will of course have been bestowed to rival parties in the past. To argue that this history renders those votes somehow invalid is to turn the process on its head.

Elections are not won on the votes of diehard party loyalists and constituencies with rock-solid majorities – such as South West Surrey or Tunbridge Wells for the Conservatives, West Ham or Bootle for Labour. It is in the so-called marginal seats – which are apt to change hands – that parliamentary majorities are built. Thus it is a given that voters who have changed party hold the key.

Then there is the phenomenon called tactical voting. My own vote in the 2015 election was a typical tactical vote. In my constituency of Chippenham, the Labour candidate was a delightful man, a local resident determined never to leave in search of a more winnable seat. But he was not going to win in Chippenham, which was held by the Liberal Democrats. I voted Lib Dem because there seemed to me to be a danger that the Conservatives would gain the seat and this would be as bad news for Labour as for the Lib Dems. The Tories did indeed take the seat and all other West Country seats except one. Now if, in verifying my application to vote in the Labour leadership election, the Labour Party had been able to discover how I had voted in May, I might have been excluded as a Lib Dem entryist, particularly if the NEC were hoping to reduce the number of ballots cast for Jeremy Corbyn by any means. This would have been most unjust. Tactical voting does not negate my support of the Labour Party.

Despite all the alarums and excursions, Corbyn's campaign serenely played out to its climax. A candidacy that barely scraped the requisite number of nominations swelled to a movement. More than 16,000 volunteers were recruited. Those working the phone banks ranged in age from thirteen to 92. There were 99 rallies, the hundredth being the coronation on September 12th.

When, at the end of August, it became clear that only intervention by the party would deny Corbyn victory, Owen Jones wrote: "I originally felt that if he came third, that would in itself be a huge political achievement. The big contribution of Jeremy's campaign, I felt, would be to put policies on the agenda, shift the terms of debate, and help rebuild a grassroots left movement; that this achievement could be built on, and crucially used to shift public opinion ... But obviously the thing about history is that it doesn't unfold in ways that you can control"[90].

Had the Tories not won their universally unpredicted overall majority in the general election of May 2015, and had Ed Miliband not promptly stepped down from leadership of the Labour Party, and had the Campaign Group put forward someone other than Jeremy Corbyn as its champion in the ensuing leadership election, the political landscape in Britain would now look very different. It demonstrates decisively that categorical assertions about what the future holds are a fool's game.

90 Medium website [August 29th 2015]

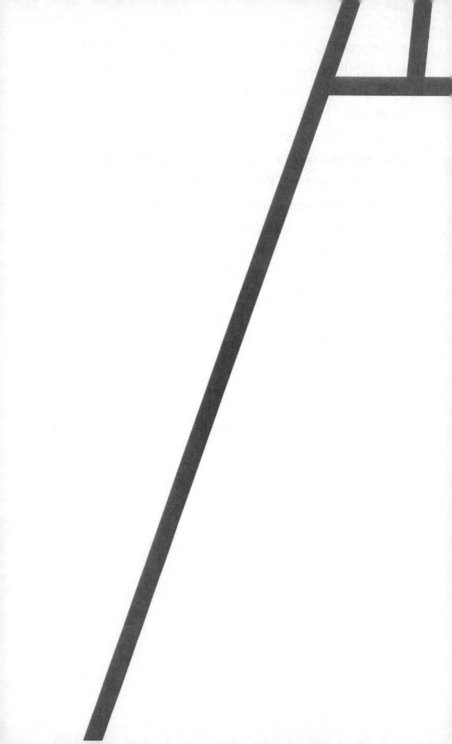

CHAPTER 3: INELUCTABLE

"Why, sometimes I've believed as many as six impossible things before breakfast" declares the Red Queen in *Through the Looking- Glass*[91]. The commentator Gary Younge quoted this at the outset of Corbyn's first week as party leader. Younge continued: "By lunchtime on Saturday that number would have been fast approaching double figures. The left-wing stalwart Jeremy Corbyn won Labour's leadership election. His first act as leader would be to address a huge rally welcoming refugees"[92].

No one could disagree that the rise of Corbyn was unpredicted and unprecedented. I noted earlier that my late mother would not have heard of Sir John Major two-and-a-half years before he became Prime Minister. Outside the Westminster village, few would have known the name Corbyn, save for residents of Islington and the odd politics geek, as recently as Easter 2015. Yet in a four-way contest for the party leadership, he won on the first ballot, with almost 60 per cent of the vote, three times that

91 *Through the Looking-Glass, and What Alice Found There* by Lewis Carroll [1871]
92 *The Guardian* [September 14th 2015]

of Andy Burnham, his nearest rival. Not even Tony Blair, with two rivals to be leader, scored so highly. No leader of any political party in British history has enjoyed such a mandate.

But change was already in the wind. Politicians from outside the centrist consensus have been gathering strong support across Europe. Syriza (otherwise known as the Coalition of the Radical Left) formed as a party in May 2012 and came into government in Greece in January 2015. Podemos ("We can") was only founded in March 2014, two months ahead of sending five socialists to the European Parliament. At the time of writing, it has become the second largest party in Spain. Over some forty years, the Front National has gathered support, culminating in 2014 in the first election win for a party opposed to the European Union in French history. The FN took 24 of the 74 French seats in the European Parliament and the mayoralties of twelve cities. In Germany, neo-Nazi grouping the Nationaldemokratische Partei Deutschlands (NPD) has taken seats in state parliaments and, since 2014, is represented by one member in the European Parliament. And in the US, Bernie Sanders and Donald Trump have shaken the respective races to be Democrat and Republican presidential candidates.

In his indispensable book *The Establishment*, columnist Owen Jones explains 'the Overton Window'[93], "a concept invented by US conservatives to describe what is deemed politically possible at any given time" and he goes on to illustrate its application: "This 'window' is relentlessly policed. So when Labour's [then leader] Ed Miliband proposes a temporary energy price freeze – a welcome, albeit pretty unremarkable, policy – it is portrayed by media and right-wing politicians as crypto-Marxism, even though most voters support a far more radical option: renationalising the energy industry lock, stock and barrel"[94].

Since Jones wrote his book, the Overton Window has palpably shifted; indeed it has slipped its moorings of being "relentlessly policed". It has been realigned by energy rising from the political grass roots. The old habits of the media have yet to adjust to this momentous change, however. It is politicking – who's up, who's down – rather than politics that is still the first subject of reporting.

In the *Guardian* issue from which I drew Gary Younge's remarks above, Professor James Curran framed a powerful argument: "Teaching

93 "Joseph P Overton [was] the late vice-president of the right-wing think-tank the Mackinac Center for Public Policy" *The Establishment* Owen Jones [pp 44-45 Allen Lane 2014]. Jones has been JC's main prophet in the press. I call him Jones the Baptist

94 *ibid* [Foreword to the Penguin edition p xviii 2015]

at Goldsmiths[95], it has been plain for some time that there has been a rising tide of political resentment reflected in social media networking, demonstrations and packed meetings. It just had no focus until Corbyn came along.

"The irony (and the untold press story) is that many young Corbyn supporters are not particularly left-wing. In the case of my students, they face an insecure job future, enormous debts and soaring rents. Yet no one seemed to be paying attention to their predicament, and addressing their concerns.

"It is a measure of political journalists' disconnection from ordinary life that they have been surprised by what has happened. If they report Corbyn's success solely through the prism of Westminster politics, it will mean they are still not paying attention to what is happening outside it"[96].

Ahead of the Labour Party Conference, Corbyn recorded a short video address for YouTube that was particularly aimed at Labour's new young recruits and was perfectly pitched to the purpose. He offered "a fantastic journey". Corbyn is sometimes accounted 'elderly' – the BBC's James Landale said so ahead of his speech to conference[97] – and watching this kindly, heartfelt

95 Goldsmiths, University of London, is a so-called "public research university" that specialises in the arts, design, humanities and social sciences
96 Letters, *The Guardian* [September 14th 2015]
97 *Daily Politics* BBC [September 29th 2015]. As someone almost exactly two years older than Corbyn, I do not feel elderly in the slightest

address I could see a rarely played role up ahead for him: Father of the Nation. It's not so far-fetched.

Once the initial impact of Corbyn's win had been remarked, the whole focus of media coverage was on the way the cast of supporting characters was changing and may still change further. The BBC's coverage of the leadership vote excitedly ran a "breaking news" strapline announcing that a junior Labour spokesman had already 'resigned', a person no viewer had heard of and whose name I have already forgotten. For days after, what passed for news was intense speculation on who would be appointed to Corbyn's team, who would refuse to serve, who would join in any perceived rebellion, how long unity would prevail. It is as though actual policy is too dull or difficult to discuss. Such soap opera dramatics preoccupies those whose lives are passed entirely in the gossipy Westminster bubble, and very few others. In the old proverb, the Westminster-watchers can't see the wood for the trees.

There was more trivia on the BBC News coverage of Corbyn's first appearance at the House's Wednesday noontime ritual, Prime Minister's Questions, which traditionally packs the chamber and is led by the Leader of the Opposition. Corbyn had sought questions from the public to put to Cameron; an amazing 40,000-odd were submitted. He put some of these using the questioner's first name, but rather than reflecting the substance of (more than one of) these questions, the news editor turned the first names into a montage, as though the audience needed to hear five to get the point.

Worse was immediately to follow. "So what do voters make of this new style of PMQs and what's the verdict on Jeremy Corbyn's first appearance?" Fiona Bruce enquired. "Our correspondent Jon Kay is in Plymouth. Jon, what's the reaction been there?" "Very, very mixed, Fiona," declared Kay emphatically. "Some people told us they couldn't get past the beard, others say that the whole thing looked like a breath of fresh air". This viewer found it difficult to get past the worse-than-tabloid news values.

Kay put to Plymouth people such compelling questions as "Do you feel like you know him?" and "Is he reaching out to you?"[98] These kinds of *vox pops* on news bulletins are mere time-fillers. Randomly coerced views on politicians years away from an election say nothing about the politicians, who cannot be blamed if a passer-by has nothing coherent to say about them.

---

98 September 16th 2015

The matter of unity is significant, though. The number of former shadow ministers returning to the backbenches is unprecedented. This alone gives force to their tactic. Whether they are able to justify their decision to anyone else's satisfaction is another matter. *The Guardian* published my letter: "When Jeremy Corbyn first declared his candidacy as Labour leader – and especially when his polling figures started to rise – it was said that he was putting ideology before party. Now that he has won a thumping victory in a brilliant show of democracy and of what the Labour party actually wants, several former frontbenchers have said they won't serve in the shadow cabinet, although (I hope I'm not being too pernickety) they've not actually been invited to do so. Just explain to me again: who is it putting ideology before party?"[99]

The 'rebels' have a case that is difficult to make sympathetic. The vote Corbyn received was overwhelming and it was produced by the most democratic election process that Labour has ever conducted; indeed, had it been less exacting, Corbyn's margin of victory would certainly have been even higher. The new leader himself has sat on the backbenches for 32 years, at odds with his party leadership on countless issues yet never a 'refusenik' – he was never invited. If he could stay

99 Letters [September 14th 2015]

in the party and fight his corner, why do some of his opponents already talk of leaving altogether?

Having refused to serve, how should they play it next? Do they just wait and see? Some of them, especially the ambitious ones, will soon grow restless. Should they quit the House, precipitating by-elections that might reaffirm Corbyn's appeal? If they have lucrative careers to go to in the city or the private health sector or the defence industry – moves which, even after all these years, are still shocking when undertaken by former Labour ministers – they probably won't give a damn about the future of the Party that allowed them to become attractive to private enterprise.

Should they stay and work to undermine and eventually (or perhaps more urgently) bring down Corbyn? This too is a risky strategy. It might fatally damage his successor or usurper. If he were replaced by Cooper or Burnham before the next election, the Tories would say that the new Labour leader couldn't even get elected in the party so why would the country be impressed?

If David Miliband were rushed in at a by-election simply to replace Corbyn as a supposedly electable leader, the term 'carpetbagger' would be forever attached to him. As for the stabbing-in-the-back legend, that would be turned on its head. Moreover, the half-buried issue of 'extraordinary rendition', on which Miliband has yet to be fully candid, would return with a vengeance.

However it falls, the Blairites need to be smart. Unless they are to reveal themselves as pure opportunists, they will not join the Tories or the Liberal Democrat rump. The Lib Dems' leader, Tim Farron, claimed that Corbyn's win opened up "a massive space in the centre ground of British politics" but then presented a sketchy version of his world view that differed in no fundamental way from Corbyn's[100]. It was hardly a pitch for disaffected Blairites.

So will the naysayers leave and found a new party? The challenge would be to find a niche between existing parties. The impact of the SDP, for which success proved fitful until it bowed to the inevitable and merged with the Liberals, is unlikely to be replicable. And no MP who left to join the SDP held ministerial office again.

In any case, the absence of Blairites in the Labour Party would allow Corbyn to carry a greater portion of his preferred programme. The more parties that ranged themselves against a Corbynite Labour Party, the greater would be the division of votes between them. But if they stay, the anti-Corbynites will need to rock the boat carefully.

100 'For Lib Dems, everything has changed', *The Guardian* [September 17th 2015]. I call him Tim Dim-But-Not-All-That-Nice

New leaders, especially those with a significant mandate, are entitled to be given a chance to deploy that mandate. Soon enough there will be opportunity to test Labour's new appeal at the ballot box – in the Holyrood and local elections in May 2016 and then the EU referendum across the UK, if not at a by-election.

Before that, opinion polling will be used to argue that Corbyn is a flop if Labour is anything less than far ahead of the Conservatives in popular esteem. Not a week after his election, *The Independent* doomily reported Labour support at around thirty per cent[101]. My reading is that one-in-three repudiated the ferociously orchestrated campaign against Corbyn in the press, a hearteningly sound base on which to build support over the months to come.

How big a gamble would it be for a disenchanted former front-bencher to change parties? After Douglas Carswell and Mark Feckless did so in the last parliament, submitting themselves successfully as UKIP candidates in the east-coast constituencies that they had hitherto represented as Conservatives, such a turncoat from Labour would be ridiculed if she did not similarly submit to a test of the water by precipitating a by-election. But such a course is fraught with danger. The

101 September 19th 2015

member running under different colours could rely neither on sufficient revulsion towards the member's former party nor on sufficient attraction to the joined party nor on an obediently transferred personal following. Even Chuka Umunna with his huge majority could not be sure what proportion of the Streatham electorate would be swayed by his own charms and what by loyalty to the Labour Party.

Besides, a premature party split would mean that the split itself would be the only aspect of Labour that voters judged, a nasty taste for the floor-crosser to leave behind. Indeed, there would be a real danger that the only beneficiary would be the Tories, thus defeating the whole object of the exercise. The prediction that carries much more conviction than that of Corbyn's unelectability is that a party riven by internal strife is unelectable.

Even so, the media gathered in Brighton for the first Labour Party Conference under Corbyn with the narrative already written. The watchword was 'dissent'. Polly Toynbee – still unforgiven by old Labour hands for transferring her column's allegiance to the SDP all those years ago – conceded: "We assembled in Brighton for a bloodbath, for gunpowder plots, sectarian skulduggery and the starting pistol fired for the great Labour civil war". But she had to report that: "It didn't happen ... The press room is dazed, confused and feeling cheated – though most deliver the headlines they'd pre-cooked anyway"[102]. There you have it, an eye-witness account from the front line of just how the media skews it, having made up their minds irrespective of the evidence.

By then we had already been treated to the mind-set of the BBC's new political editor, Laura Kuenssberg, in reporting the Conference speech of John McDonnell. "He couldn't resist a swipe at those senior MPs who don't want to be part of the project", she declared. Here's what McDonnell actually said: "I admit I was disappointed after Jeremy's election that some people refused to serve. In the spirit of solidarity upon which our movement was founded, I say 'Come back, come back and help us succeed'."[103] On what planet would such a direct and wholly unconditional invitation be deemed "a swipe"?

It would be idle to pretend, however, that such dissent had wholly melted away. "All we've seen is conflict deferred," pronounced the aforementioned John 'Morons' McTernan[104]; just as old ministers go and join what they used to pretend were the

---

102 *The Guardian* [September 29th 2015]
103 BBC Television News [September 28th 2015]
104 *Newsnight* BBC2 [September 28th 2015]

'enemy' private enterprise, so he now writes for *The Telegraph*. Another former Blair advisor describing himself as from "the moderate wing", Lance Price, immediately tore into Corbyn's speech with a venom that a Tory frontbencher might have baulked at[105], but it was plain that he was predisposed to do so, that if he had slipped off to the BBC Club while the speech was broadcast he would have come back and said nothing different.

The likes of McTernan and Price are the proxies for those former frontbenchers who declined to serve, the ones who hesitate to be seen to be decrying Corbyn until a propitious moment but who want to keep discontent bubbling without being blamed for their disloyalty and anti-democratic manoeuvrings.

McTernan and Price both make the point that "All the party's been doing is talking to itself"[106]. McTernan said that if Corbyn and McDonnell "do any listening to voters, they'll come back talking about immigration, welfare, and the economy and borrowing, and I don't think we're seeing listening, we're seeing people talking to the party" (presenter

105 *Daily Politics* BBC2 [September 29th 2015]. It was hard to see the famous BBC 'balance' in operation here. After Tim Farron's leader's speech to the Lib Dem Conference, the guest commentator was a party enthusiast. Price was the only voice in the studio after Corbyn's "absolutely dreadful" speech and was so *parti pris* that Andrew Neil, surely against his own instincts, was obliged to defend Corbyn. You will know if I was right, gentle reader, but I bet that the coverage of David Cameron's Conference speech [given after this book had gone to the printers] will not have starred a comparable Cameron foe
106 *Ibid*

Evan Davis asked "Have you had any change of view at all?" and fellow guest Zoë Williams smartly interjected "In twenty years?")[107].

It's reasonable to question on what evidence McTernan bases his assessment of public concern and whether he can seriously claim to have interacted with a cross-section of the public this year remotely as wide as has the Corbyn campaign, in both general and leadership elections. His issues list reads to me like media-fed presumption.

In Corbyn's first days as party leader, it was all improvisation and gut reaction, often heedless of how this might play with the media through which the electorate would perceive it. That the press would be hostile and the broadcast reporting (probably artlessly) biased – in, for instance, habitually characterising him as a 'left-winger' – was the one element of Corbyn's transition that could have been fully anticipated and hence planned for by him or at least his advisors.

This seems not to have happened, or else Corbyn declined to play that game. I think it was an opportunity missed. There will obviously be times when Corbyn's instinct needs to be tempered by realists. In his victory speech, Corbyn thanked his many personal friends in the Islington North party "and I absolutely value their advice. Sometimes it's advice you don't always want to receive, but that's the best advice you get"[108]. He repeated the point at Brighton. And he needs to cleave to that.

How things pan out depends more than usually on the demeanour of the leader himself. Corbyn talks always about democracy and of carrying people with him rather than imposing on them. But it is inevitable that he will sometimes have to crack the whip if he is not just going to roll over and embrace policies he deplores rather than spark dissent. Not on everything will he be able to offer a free vote in the Commons. But he will need to choose his targets cunningly.

In his public appearances, there is no sense of timetable or scale, no hint of rapprochement and no guile. Every statement, every speech is like a campaign engagement. Corbyn never seems to be in the business of persuading doubters but in reinforcing fixed positions. He has no experience of management or diplomacy, only of advocacy and opposition. And it shows.

Clearly Conservative ministers sit back and grin, believing that all they have to do is to watch amateur night empty the hall. But wiser heads counsel caution. Ken Clarke, an MP even longer (by thirteen years) than Corbyn, warned his party to be careful what they wished for long before the new

---

108 *Op cit*

Labour leader was unveiled. "Don't underestimate Jeremy Corbyn," he told *The Huffington Post*. "He's a nice guy. It's not certain he will lose an election. Michael Foot, who stood on a much more left-wing platform in 1983, was miles ahead before the election. If you have another recession or if the Conservative government becomes very unpopular, he could win. In difficult times, the party with the duty of government can become unpopular. He will be difficult to campaign against.

"Corbyn fits the bill of being anti-political. He's regarded as a non-politician's answer to the Westminster establishment. Labour activists are very attracted to him because he sounds and looks like he believes what he says"[109]. The implied contrast to Clarke's leader David Cameron is noted.

It was inevitable that the media spotlight would focus on Corbyn's conduct until such time as a more compelling story came along. But aside from those moments for which the reporters lay in wait – those moments that they could use against him with the electorate – the rest of the principal casting seemed all that the political reporter or columnist watched and assessed.

With his pick of potential shadow ministers haemorrhaging to the backbenches, Corbyn

---

109 August 3rd 2015

inevitably took many hours to put together a government in waiting. He had declared that the sexes would be balanced in his team, but several leading women – Mary Creagh, Shabana Mahmood, Rachel Reeves, Emma Reynolds, Caroline Flint and his defeated rivals Yvette Cooper and Liz Kendall – all declined to be available for consideration. Nevertheless. Corbyn came up with a shadow cabinet of fifteen men and sixteen women, an unprecedented feat. Far from hailing this as a breakthrough, however, the pedants seized on men – John McDonnell, Hilary Benn, Andy Burnham – being appointed to shadow the Treasury, the Foreign Office and the Home Office.

"The appointment of only men to shadow the great offices of state projected an attitude to equal gender representation that was complacent at best," fussed columnist Rafael Behr. "The defence that 'great offices of state' is itself an archaic construct was old-fashioned spin"[110]. I suggest that you could go years without coming across the phrase "great offices of state" in the papers. Nobody beyond Westminster and academe has any use for it.

Heidi Alexander, Corbyn's shadow Secretary of State for Health, pointed out that those with the health and education portfolios – Lucy Powell

110 *The Guardian* [September 16th 2015]

shadows education – directly touch rather more lives in Britain than do the supposed 'leading roles'[111]. Indeed, I doubt that significantly more lay people could identify the present Foreign Secretary than the Health Secretary (respectively, Philip Hammond and Jeremy Hunt).

Another 'controversial' front-bench appointment, that of Kerry McCarthy, prompted this observation from Stewart Lee: "He was mocked for making a vegan shadow Environment Secretary. Yet under David Cameron we have an Equalities Minister who was against equal marriage, an anti-environmentalist Environment Secretary, and a Culture Secretary who loves torture porn and wants to dismantle the BBC"[112]. These parish-pump matters are presented as defining 'blunders' in order to establish the myth that Corbyn is an incompetent.

For Conservatives, the most pressing motive to keep Corbyn out of office – and the myth of incompetence worked devastatingly to this end against Foot, Kinnock and Miliband – is the public finances and Corbyn's contrary approach to them, what is already being called Corbynomics. No bones have been made about where the new Labour leader stands: it is on "a clear anti-austerity

111 *The World at One* interview, BBC Radio 4 [September 14th 2015]
112 *The Observer* [September 20th 2015]. Of course, one can never be entirely sure when Lee is joking

platform", confirmed both by Corbyn and by his enemies.

It isn't so much that the government and its supporters think savage cuts in public services and welfare are highly popular, but rather that these policies are presented as necessary and the only choice for a sensible regime. Cameron and Osborne bank on the electorate not knowing that increasing numbers of economists take issue with austerity as a necessity or even as a wise approach.

Among those now ranged against them are the Nobel laureates Joseph Stiglitz and Paul Krugman as well as the achingly fashionable Thomas Piketty. Here is Krugman, writing shortly before the 2015 election: "All of the economic research that allegedly supported the austerity push has been discredited. Widely touted statistical results were, it turned out, based on highly dubious assumptions and procedures – plus a few outright mistakes – and evaporated under closer scrutiny. It is rare, in the history of economic thought, for debates to get resolved this decisively. The austerian ideology that dominated elite discourse five years ago has collapsed, to the point where hardly anyone still believes it. Hardly anyone, that is, except the coalition that still rules Britain – and most of the British media".

Krugman also recorded how the austerity mantra spread across the political spectrum on both sides of the Atlantic, especially the holy ground of the political centre: "Conservatives like to use the alleged dangers of debt and deficits as clubs with which to beat the welfare state and justify cuts in benefits; suggestions that higher spending might actually be beneficial are definitely not welcome. Meanwhile, centrist politicians and pundits often try to demonstrate how serious and statesmanlike they are by calling for hard choices and sacrifice (by other people). Even Barack Obama's first inaugural address, given in the face of a plunging economy, largely consisted of hard-choices boilerplate. As a result, centrists were almost as uncomfortable with the notion of fiscal stimulus as the hard right".

Thus Cameron and Osborne, lamely followed by Ed Miliband and his shadow Chancellor Ed Balls, convinced themselves that fiscal parsimony was the only cure for the damage done by the global recession of 2008-09 and they used the facile metaphor of the family finances to sell the idea to the electorate.

But of course national economies are nothing like household budgets. Here is Paul Krugman again: "The doctrine that ruled the world in 2010 has more or less vanished from the scene. Except in Britain ... The 'primary purpose' of austerity, the *Telegraph* admitted in 2013, 'is to shrink the size of government spending'[113] – or, as Cameron put it in a speech later that year, to make the state 'leaner ... not just now, but permanently'[114] ... Britain's opposition has been amazingly willing to accept claims that budget deficits are the biggest economic issue facing the nation, and has made hardly any effort to challenge the extremely dubious proposition that fiscal policy under Blair and Brown was deeply irresponsible – or even the nonsensical proposition that this supposed fiscal irresponsibility caused the crisis of 2008-09".

And so Krugman explains pithily why the kind of jump-start to the public finances that Corbyn envisages is exactly the constructive course to take: "An economy that is depressed even with zero interest rates is, in effect, an economy in which the public is trying to save more than businesses are willing to invest. In such an economy the government does everyone a service by running deficits and giving frustrated savers a chance to put their money to work. Nor does this borrowing compete with private investment. An economy where interest rates cannot go any

---

113 Jeremy Warner [September 11th 2013]
114 Lord Mayor's Banquet [November 11th 2013]

lower is an economy awash in desired saving with no place to go, and deficit spending that expands the economy is, if anything, likely to lead to higher private investment than would otherwise materialise ... I often encounter people on both the left and the right who imagine that austerity policies were what the textbook said you should do – that those of us who protested against the turn to austerity were staking out some kind of heterodox, radical position. But the truth is that mainstream, textbook economics not only justified the initial round of post-crisis stimulus, but said that this stimulus should continue until economies had recovered.

"What we got instead, however, was a hard right turn in elite opinion, away from concerns about unemployment and toward a focus on slashing deficits, mainly with spending cuts"[115].

In his Brighton conference speech, John McDonnell had a line doubtless intended for quotation: "Austerity is not an economic necessity, it's a political choice"[116]. It's a line that Corbyn's Labour Party will use again and again, I suspect. Krugman wasn't mentioned, but McDonnell announced the setting up of an Economic Advisory

115 'The Austerity Delusion' *The Guardian* [April 29th 2015]. I feel sure that, in choosing his title for the essay, Krugman intended to evoke Richard Dawkins' celebrated assault on supernatural fallacies, *The God Delusion* [Bantam 2006]
116 September 28th 2015

Committee to help the Party, its members including Mariana Mazzucato, David Blanchflower, Ann Pettifor and Simon Wren-Lewis, as well as Stiglitz and Piketty. This was little remarked, but it is hugely suggestive of Labour's new ambition to be bold and imaginative in getting the economy right. These advisors could have as far-reaching an effect in developing Corbynomics as Friedrich Hayek, Milton Friedman and Alan Walters had in the creation of Thatcherism.

More compelling for Laura Kuenssberg was that "There was precious little detail of the tax rises or cuts that might be required"[117] as though McDonnell had let the Party down by failing to unveil the 2020 election manifesto right away. The expectation – or the pretence of expectation – that all the answers ought to be ready immediately is a widespread stance in the media.

Corbyn and McDonnell had previously indicated that they favour a new round of the expansionary technique called Quantitative Easing, which is to say the injection of new money into the public finances. Under Mervyn King's governorship of the Bank of England, the Monetary Policy Committee (which determines interest rates and other monetary levels) financed £375 billion worth of government debt. The Corbynomics version of this

117 BBC News

gambit is referred to as the People's Quantitative Easing, Corbyn and McDonnell intending it to seed growth in the economy, particularly the manufacturing side, rather than to prop up the banks and other institutions in financial services.

Jeremy Warner explodes at the notion: "Of all Mr Corbyn's crackpot policies, 'People's QE' is by far the most dangerous, for if implemented unchecked it would almost inevitably lead to a collapse in the currency and eventually the kind of hyper-inflation that engulfed Weimar Germany. More recent examples include such notable paragons of economic success as Zimbabwe and Argentina"[118].

Who says it would be implemented unchecked? American academic Benjamin Studebaker, recently at Queen's, Cambridge, declares: "Corbyn should be taken seriously – those who oppose him must be made to engage with the optimal tax rate literature and they must be made to engage with what we've learned from the QE experience. The flippant dismissal we're seeing of Corbyn and his ideas should not be allowed to pass unchecked"[119]. And 42 other academics, mostly economists, wrote to *The Guardian* to dispute the characterisation of Corbyn's economic policies as "extreme ... Despite the barrage of media coverage to the contrary, it is

118 *The Daily Telegraph* [August 21st 2015]
119 His blog [August 5th 2015]

the current government's policy and its objectives which are extreme"[120].

As it happens, McDonnell has rowed back from the foregrounding of QE, having been persuaded that it works best as a policy for a falling rather than a rising economy. He said in Brighton: "As a start I have invited Lord Bob Kerslake, former head of the civil service, to bring together a team to review the operation of the Treasury itself. I will also be setting up a review of the Bank of England. Let me be clear that we will guarantee the independence of the Bank of England.

"It is time though to open a debate on the Bank's mandate that was set by Parliament 18 years ago. The mandate focuses on inflation, and even there the Bank regularly fails to meet its target. We will launch a debate on expanding that mandate to include new objectives for its Monetary Policy Committee including growth, employment and earnings. We will review the operation and resourcing of Her Majesty's Revenue & Customs to ensure that HMRC is capable of addressing tax evasion and avoidance and modernising our tax collection system. This is how we will prepare for the future and the day we return to government"[121]. In anyone's language, this is constructive thinking.

120 Letters to the editor [August 23rd 2015]
121 Brighton Conference speech [September 28th 2015]

All the attacks on Corbynomics are couched in apocalyptic terms; five minutes after McDonnell arrives in the Treasury, we will all be living in cardboard boxes (whereas now, of course, it is only the 'work-shy' who live like that). Here's a view from thriller novelist Matthew Lynn who, in 2007, declared that Apple "will sell a few to its fans, but the iPhone won't make a long-term mark on the industry"[122]: "The trouble is, the policies on offer under Corbynomics would quickly ruin the economy. Take tuition fees. Corbyn has proposed scrapping them and making university education free again, just as it is in Scotland. How will that be paid for? He has suggested a 7% rise in national insurance contributions for those earning more than £50,000 a year and a 2% rise in corporation tax. That would be a huge tax rise on people on relatively modest incomes – if you have a family to support, £50,000 hardly makes you Roman Abramovich.

"And if the UK started raising corporation tax, it would be about the only country in the world to do so – hardly a way to attract investment ... He campaigns against austerity, much as the SNP does, conveniently ignoring the fact that by any historical standards the UK is already running a huge budget deficit. In his world, governments can

122 *Bloomberg* [January 14th 2007]

spend more than they raise in taxes forever. At the same time, he would strengthen trade union rights, weaken the power of private companies to run their own affairs, and increase the size of the public sector"[123].

Readers may judge how far the items in the last sentence are undesirable. But the idea that £50,000 a year is "relatively modest" shows that Lynn knows nothing of ordinary lives. £26,500 is the average salary in Britain. Four in five of new 40-hour week jobs are in sectors averaging below £16,640. A full-time job at the hourly minimum wage pays £13,124. Even architects, barristers and financial advisors average below £50,000[124]. The figure of £50,000 signifies because it is where the Tories want to have set the higher rate tax threshold by the next election. The projected loss in tax revenue for the year 2019-20 that would be required to allow this handout to the wealthy would be £1.68 billion.[125]

Tax is an issue that Tories and Socialists view very differently. The rich man resents losing noticeable amounts of his income to the "public good". He doesn't use the education, health care and transport provided by the state. He grumbles that the lanes to his country estate are all pot-

123 *MoneyWeek* [July 26th 2015]
124 Office of National Statistics figures, quoted by the *Daily Mirror* [March 31st 2015]
125 *This Is Money* website [March 18th 2015]

holes, police are tardy when poaching is detected on his land and courts make him wait when his tenants defy his eviction order, but he can't see that cuts in government spending touch on those things. He feels he has a moral duty to hand to his children the style in which they have been raised and if he has to live at his overseas address for a certain portion of the year to safeguard the family wealth, it is not so dismaying a duty. But he expects those ministers whom he knows socially and their friends with whom he serves on company boards to play the game.

Her Majesty's Revenue & Customs has revealed that nearly seven per cent of all taxes due in the financial year 2013-14 went unpaid, a total of £34 billion[126]. This amount would easily cover the quite as staggering figure of unclaimed income-related benefit in the same financial year: £24 billion. That means that every day there is £66 million of entitlement that is not taken up[127]. And still the government intends to slash the welfare budget.

In every one of his budget statements, George Osborne seems to have vowed to do something radical about tax evasion if not tax avoidance, but there is still uncollected tax sufficient exactly to

126 *Daily Mail* [October 16th 2014]
127 Figures interpreted by SPeye website based on 'Income-Related Benefits: Estimate of Take-Up' [Department for Work & Pensions document, June 25th 2015]

pay for the government's bill for public order and safety – which means in practice: the law courts, prisons, police and fire services and matters "not elsewhere classified", such as public hygiene examination; in other words, a significant amount of money.

Richard Murphy, Corbyn's economics guru, thinks HMRC's guess of £34 billion is a gross underestimate. He prefers a figure of £122 billion[128], which would comfortably pay for the entire welfare budget (currently £110.5 billion). "How is it that there are only two estimates of the tax gap, mine and the Inland Revenue's?" he asked *The Guardian*. "Nobody else has come into this major arena and done some work. I'd love it if they did".

Murphy evidently believes that taxation policy has a moral dimension, something which you can well imagine would chime with Corbyn's reformist instincts. "The joy of tax is simply the ability of tax to create the type of society we want, which I don't think anything else can", he says. "We don't live in a world which is perfect. I think that tax can be the mechanism that we use to deliver a better life for most people in the UK. If that isn't something that we should be celebrating, I don't know what is"[129].

"It's the economy, stupid" was a powerfully

---

128 *The Tax Gap* report by Richard Murphy for the Public and Commercial Services Union [2014]
129 *The Guardian* [September 23rd 2015]

effective slogan dreamed up by Bill Clinton's strategist James Carville during the 1992 election campaign in the US. It is likely to underpin Corbyn's tenure as Labour Party leader, primarily because he understands how far the party has to row back from the embedded perception that, when last in office, Labour "bankrupted the country", "failed to regulate the banks" and "didn't mend the roof when the sun was shining". To be "trusted" with the public finances has been smartly established by the Conservatives as an acid test of a political party and of course there has been a consistent and concerted effort to fix in the public mind that Labour has been found wanting on this score. Counteracting that perception and, additionally, seeing off the idea that he must be an ideological spendthrift will be a ferocious test of Corbyn's persuasive powers.

The moment he was elected, the Tories played a card that was potentially even more devastating. Cameron tweeted: "The Labour Party is now a threat to our national security, our economic security and your family's security"[130]. Of course, such a scathing attack would only do its work if people believed it. Thousands swarmed all over the message, rubbishing it comprehensively. My favourite response from those I saw was a

---

130 Twitter [September 13th 2015]

handwritten correction, scoring through everything after the words "a threat to" and writing in instead "the Tory Party". Others sent in Freedom of Information requests to call the bluff on what Cameron "knows" about Corbyn.

At Brighton, Corbyn answered Cameron's tweet with a crescendo of instances where Tory policy could be described as undermining the security of the citizenry, a virtuoso passage that set the hall on a roar. And when he castigated the Tories because "they expect millions of people to work harder longer for a lower quality of life on lower wages. Well, they're not having it. Our Labour Party says 'no'. The British people never have to take what they're given", there was a prolonged standing ovation.

The Tories also released what, in American politics, is called "an attack ad", reinforcing the notion that Corbyn represented some unspecified danger. This too backfired. The ad had to be taken down for breach of copyright.

In his Brighton speech, Corbyn projected a strong sense that politics is about self-abnegation, not as a self-serving pose but as a genuine philosophy, that one only achieves a worthwhile political attainment if it is on behalf of someone less fortunate who has need of the power and contacts that you bring as a politician. This had a particular resonance, given the absence in the hall of so many hitherto key players too self-important to risk being seen unguardedly clapping something that they might want later to forswear. Tristram Hunt and Yvette Cooper, Chuka Umunna and Rachel Reeves, Chris Leslie and Liam Byrne, Mary Creagh and Caroline Flint, Emma Reynolds and Liz Kendall are apparently more concerned with their own intriguing than with the needs of the Labour Party. They may have seriously miscalculated; the Party members will have taken note.

All this jockeying for advantage ahead of an imagined contest for a future election may well be idle and academic, however. There is a view, which I rather incline to myself, that opposition parties do not win elections, that in the (relatively unusual) case where there is a change of government it is because the party in office loses it. History seems to bear this out. Set aside 1945, a unique case because it was the first opportunity to cast a vote in a full decade, and millions of those voters were returning from service in war, a profound experience that was also clearly a politicising experience among significant numbers.

In every election since, where the incumbent was defeated, the governing party was widely seen to be intellectually bankrupt or exhausted or divided or corrupt or any combination thereof. In these cases, the opposing party came to power sometimes in spite of itself rather than owing to its exciting and encouraging appeal.

There is a further disadvantage for Labour in this reading of electoral history. The Tories are seen, largely subconsciously, as "the natural party of government", certainly by Tories themselves. After what he called "thirteen years of Tory misrule", Harold Wilson explicitly tried to overturn this perception and, for a while, it seemed that he might have done so. But within just 160 weeks of his stepping down, the Conservatives began eighteen unbroken years of government. That Tony Blair's Labour Party ended this run was more to do with the comprehensive collapse of John Major's regime than with any perceived merit in Labour.

What can Corbyn do about this? There is not much that can be initiated to undermine the obvious advantage held by the party in office; if history be a guide, he can only wait for that undermining to be achieved by Cameron and his ministers. It might be said too that few Labour leaders have set off from a position further away from a widely held view that it is a natural party of government. Here is not so much a mountain to climb as a Himalayan range.

It's also fair to observe that Corbyn can do more to help his cause. Paying no attention to media noise has its attractions. Refusing to trim to pressure or to resort to smooth words has been central to the man's appeal. But there are downsides here too. One thing that politicians are never allowed to say is "I didn't know". It may well be that some crisis is, in practical terms, impossible for the leader's team to anticipate or to pre-empt, but that cuts little ice in the unforgiving world of politics and media scrutiny. "It's your job to know" is the standard rejoinder and it is difficult to gainsay.

Leaders are expected to take responsibility for every aspect of their party's conduct of itself and every insignificant minion's unguarded remark. They are never permitted to pass such things off as the inevitable small change of sprawling organisations full of opinionated and ambitious individuals. Small embarrassments can quickly blow up into major gaffes and then rumble on for days until some sacrificial lamb is thrown to the dogs. And an approach that is consciously anti-professional carries obvious risk of mishap.

Corbyn's first weeks as leader were certainly not mishap-free, if you deem bad press a mishap. Of course, the Tory press is primed to present his every move and every word in the worst possible light. Those of us used to blizzards of propaganda wryly anticipated the sort of headlines there would be: "Corbyn eats babies", "Jezza raped my granny", "Corbyn's chum funds terror fiends". And so they came. On the day that the government made deep cuts in tax credits for hundreds of thousands of the papers' readers, the very people that ministers fawn over as "hard-working families", Corbyn attended the service at St Paul's Cathedral that marked the 75th anniversary of the Battle of Britain. When the national anthem was sung, he did not join in.

Here was the raped-my-granny moment the press had longed for. "Corbyn snubs the Queen" was the actual main headline or the gist of it on almost every newspaper. As Her Majesty was not present at the service, the claim was not exactly accurate. Though a strange word rarely heard in ordinary people's conversation, "snub" is a newspaper favourite, a neat stubby word that jumps out of a headline. Whether the enormity at St Paul's was greater or lesser than the annual ritual when Hollywood "snubs" some actor who has failed to be nominated for an Oscar is not apparent. But a snub has news value that a welfare cut does not, particularly if it is credited to a reviled enemy.

Hence the outrage was contrived rather than felt, synthetic rather than genuine. Still, in any walk of life, it's a good idea to avoid unnecessarily alienating people.

The occasion provided further ammunition for Corbyn's detractors. The arch Tory blogger Paul Staines ran a story that the Labour leader had "grabbed" sandwiches provided after the service for veterans and volunteers – "not one but two free Costa coffee lunch bags". The "story" was according to and illustrated by "respected photographer Steve Back" – respected no longer, I venture.

Nearly an hour later, Staines withdrew the allegation and apologised, having had another image uploaded that clearly showed Costa staff offering the sandwiches to Corbyn. The original mischief remains on his site doing the damage it is meant to do by catching the eye and slipping into the brain, the withdrawal tucked in below[131].

Corbyn's response is to ignore the muck-spreading, not to allow anything to ruffle him and to assume that voters will see it for the vendetta that it is. It's quite a leap of faith in people's decency. But it's a high-risk strategy. Though I suspect that the person in Westminster least likely to read this book is Corbyn himself, not knowing what is

131 Guido Fawkes website [September 15th 2015]

said about you dices with missing danger signals. Remaining oblivious to attack can shield a leader from distraction and trivial skirmishes, but it can shade into seeming detached and insensitive. It's fine for leaders to ignore the press – Ed Miliband used to deny that he looked at it – but it's essential for *someone* to monitor it daily, so that potential problems are nipped in the bud.

The Tory aim now is to put Corbyn on the back foot. In another context, Suzanne Moore quoted Hunter S Thompson on "one of the best tricks in politics ... that he'd seen ... used by Lyndon B Johnson. Johnson suggested his opponent had a penchant for 'carnal knowledge of his own barnyard sows'. His campaign manager said no one would believe it. 'I know,' Johnson replied. 'But let's make the sonofabitch deny it'."[132] For all that Corbyn is devoted to straight talking, open dealing and honest planning, he sorely needs a few Machiavels beside him to carry out the necessary tasks that would taint his own reputation if he were to execute them.

In his deputy Tom Watson, he has a past master at deploying propagandist methods effectively and leaning on people without unnecessarily alienating potential supporters. Labour needs to learn how to fight dirty and to hit back. And, in the proper

132 *The Guardian* [September 22nd 2015]

Corbyn manner, it should be absolutely open about doing so. Watson can announce: "This is what we're doing, this is why we're doing it, and this is how we're going about it".

At the same time as hitting back, Corbyn's team needs to make it crystal clear to MPs and others that political manoeuvrings within the party will not be tolerated, and that whispering campaigns and off-the-record briefings of journalists are no longer permitted. Discipline needs to be imposed through the reasonable method of demanding self-discipline from MPs.

This could not be deemed an assault on democracy or the start of a purge. After all, the concept of 'collective responsibility', which has been upheld in cabinets and their shadows as long as anyone can remember, has been pretty much abandoned, *de facto* if not formally. With his history of rebellion and readiness to argue his case openly, Corbyn could hardly clamp any version of *omertà* on his colleagues; nor does he seem unduly bothered if front-bench colleagues disagree with him or among themselves. It's all the natural operation of democracy, he seems to say.

Allowing constant debate and the free expression of dissenting views within the shadow cabinet is simultaneously a refreshing change of methodology and the price to be paid for heading off a more damaging revolt. In Brighton, Corbyn described it as "not necessarily message discipline all the time". But other parts of the Labour Party have openly encouraged discussion and dissent in the past. Alan Milburn and Charles Clarke, among the most scathing of Corbyn's critics inside the Party, set up an 'open forum' website called *The 2020 Vision*, to set "about looking to the world a decade or more ahead, about identifying the new challenges the world [will] face and the new policies needed to implement progressive values"[133].

Clarke described the aim as "to debate future policies with both the party and the public"[134], words that might have been spoken this year by Corbyn. But that was in 2007; 2020 referred to the expression used to denote perfect eyesight rather than to the date (not then known) of the next general election. The site no longer functions. Milburn went into the lucrative business of private medicine, his path conceivably eased somewhat by the experience he had gained as Secretary of State for Health. Clarke lost his seat in 2010 and now carps from a hinterland of academe and selling computers to schools.

---

133 the2020vision.org.uk
134 Quoted on World Socialist Web site [March 23rd 2007]

In attempting to engage with all parts of the Party, including those most suspicious of his motives and alarmed by his success, Corbyn is in the business of rebuilding Labour, of undoing the damage that John McDonnell reckoned had been done by the time Blair stepped down: that he had "broken up the broad coalition of support Labour has relied upon throughout its history to bring it to power ... [and had] systematically alienated section after section of our supporters"[135].

In his speech to the Brighton Conference, Corbyn projected "a kinder politics", simultaneously advocating it as an offering to the voters and requesting it from his critics. It's a thoughtful pitch, vain in the latter case no doubt but attempting to draw the teeth of his enemies' projection of him as the friend of "bad men". He'll need those who work with him to conduct themselves with continuing self-discipline, though, and he was indeed loudly applauded for castigating the abuse seen on social media. It helped to lay the ground for this appeal that he had begun his address so evidently genial, relaxed, warm and self-mockingly amusing. For my own taste, I could do without him applauding the audience. It seems to fuse the Kremlin of the 1950s with the style of present-day American showbiz, a queasy mix. And

---

135 *Ibid*

one person clapping close to a microphone requires the action to be brisk and firm or it sounds mightily half-hearted.

The style was certainly rambling. The effect was of a big *tour d'horizon*, as if he could finally say *everything* he'd wanted to say to the Party all these years but was never before allowed to. He tried to straddle the new and unaccustomed pressures and duties of his elevation and the instincts that have always guided him. At one point, he assured his supporters that "I'm not going to stop standing up on those issues or being that activist".

It is on nuclear disarmament that the reality of his lack of support in the shadow cabinet is most starkly revealed; at conference, the issue was voted off the agenda pending a policy review, but the shadow Secretary of State for Defence, Maria Eagle (who perhaps significantly in several ways was almost the last shadow appointment made), is unlikely to stop standing up on an issue on which she too feels strongly: she favours renewal of Trident.

Corbyn said he wanted to be "absolutely clear: the best way to protect the British people against the threats we face to our safety at home and abroad is to work to resolve conflict. That isn't easy but it is unavoidable if we want real security

... I don't believe that £100 bn spent on a new generation of nuclear weapons taking up a quarter of our defence budget is the right way forward". This was loudly applauded in the hall. But it will be a long drawn-out business before the issue is resolved in a way that allows Labour to take a coherent position in a Commons debate and vote. You can bet that the Tories will accelerate the matter, confident that their own party will stay together.

Many critics attacked Corbyn for the things he didn't say in his address. There is a constant demand in the media for a public *post mortem* on the general election result. Margaret Beckett is in the process of conducting such an exercise and gave an interim report at the conference, but at that time the media were doubtless busy hunting dissent at fringe meetings. To my knowledge, no one has offered any evidence that there is any discernible demand from the electorate that the election be raked over. It feels like an attempt by the Tory press to extract some "confession" that can then be used against Labour in the 2020 election campaign.

It's just as tangential that McDonnell's speech on the economy evidently left them wanting more from Corbyn. But the main reason for these objections is tied up with the style of modern reporting. For several days before the speech, both print and broadcast coverage were preoccupied with speculation and presumptuous previewing of what Corbyn was going to say. This begins to function like the anticipation of the Oscars or the Booker Prize, so that when there is a "different" result, the judges must be castigated for defying the conventional wisdom.

The other thread of criticism was that the speech did not constitute an election-ready manifesto. The 24-hour news cycle requires that complete answers be given right now to every question, tomorrow being too late because the circus will have left town. That politics is a long-form art is of little interest to reporters and commentators. That's for the documentarists and the historians. Politicians are required to be the complete package now and every day.

"Much of what Corbyn said in Brighton was about campaigning differently," reported Jonathan Freedland, "as if that were an end in itself. Governing, power – almost seemed secondary"[136]. But at this stage of the political cycle, they *are* secondary. Labour's present job is to oppose the government, to function as Her Majesty's Opposition, not yet to present itself as a

136 *The Guardian* [September 30th 2015]

government in waiting. And campaigning is a more positive and creative and eye-catching stance than mere opposing. It allows the opposition to initiate and to lead the discussion. How is that wrong?

This phony urgency also shapes the way that politicians are interviewed. Martha Kearney of *The World at One* frequently harangues frontbenchers over their latest opinion poll figures as if the survival of the planet depends on it. That the opinion polls couldn't get close to projecting the result of the 2015 general election even on polling day is conveniently forgotten. Now some phone poll of a couple of thousand people, self-selected by being available and willing to take part, is offered as if it is what clinches the eternal fate of an entire political movement. This is politics as action movie rather than analysis.

Politicians should flatly refuse to address opinion poll findings and indeed to answer hypothetical questions. "Would you press the nuclear button?" is an absurd question, asked of Corbyn on the BBC[137]. Would you knife a burglar? Evidently, the inference must be that, if you wouldn't, you will be burgled forthwith, even all killed in your beds. No other leader anywhere in the world is asked this question. Would Cameron press the button? Would Farron,

---

137 *Today*, Radio 4 [September 30th 2015]

140

Farage, Obama, Hollande, Putin, Netanyahu? If any of them answered 'yes', that would amount to a declaration of war. And there would have to be follow-up questions: How many casualties would be unacceptable? What would you have done to guard against retaliation? What guarantees could you give that areas beyond the target would be unaffected? Unless the issue is properly explored, it's just a tasteless after-dinner game. If this is the big test for Corbyn's survival as Labour leader, let everyone else, including all Labour frontbenchers, undertake the same test.

The Corbyn experiment may still end with him destroyed by the Tory press or with Labour rendered unelectable, fulfilling the fate intended by the press. But remember that endorsement on Twitter by Rupert Murdoch, who is certainly no fool. Sometimes people who would customarily behave as enemies intuit that they may prosper if they explore other avenues. Richard Nixon flew to Beijing to meet Mao Zedong. Margaret Thatcher said of Mikhail Gorbachev: "I like Mr Gorbachev; we can do business together". Jeremy Corbyn may yet prove to be a man who changes the world.

Meanwhile, party hacks and the media commentariat tell us daily and with breathtaking confidence what Corbyn will do or will fail to do and what the electorate will do or will fail to do.

The morning after Corbyn's election, Janet Daley wrote: "One of two things will happen. Either the Parliamentary Labour Party will go momentarily quiescent while it regroups, refusing co-operation and advice to the leadership clique. Or else the Corbyn crew[138] will be brought down within months by a Labour assassination squad. This will result in a decade of division within the party – but the hard Left will be particularly scarred by the viciousness of its fight to the death"[139]. So there it is. The oracle has pronounced. No other eventuality is possible. Why the future should have been revealed to Janet Daley rather than, say, Arthur Daley I cannot explain. But it was surprising that she neglected to anticipate 'Piggate'.

Initially, some did hesitate a day or so. Even Rafael Behr conceded that "There are no safe predictions any more" (though you can guess that the next word was "but")[140]. This didn't last. Speculation and prediction long ago replaced news-reporting as the chief function of newspapers and that is not going to be changed by a realignment of domestic politics. Doom scenarios can take on the characteristics of a campaign and eventually gain a momentum that overwhelms all

138 These loaded terms (clique, crew) are always used about Labour. Blair's team were habitually called "Tony's cronies" in the Tory press
139 *The Daily Telegraph* [September 13th 2015]
140 *The Guardian* [September 16th 2015]

other perceptions in the public mind. The result is a self-fulfilling prophecy: no other resolution is possible because every other possibility has been comprehensively discounted. This is exactly what Corbyn's foes, within and without the Labour Party, intend.

His supporters must exercise eternal vigilance. Edmund Burke is the orator-politician most often credited with the powerful observation that "All that is necessary for the triumph of evil is that good men do nothing"[141]. Those who, inspired by his campaign, flooded into the Labour movement must apply their energies both to fending off orchestrated attacks upon his conduct and reputation and to keeping him up to the high mark that he has set himself.

All politicians prove a disappointment. The daily grind of striving to be consistent and effective tempers intent and theory. RA Butler hit the bullseye when he called politics "the art of the possible". But there is no inevitability about the failure and/or the coup that all the cynics, malcontents and commentators presume will engulf Jeremy Corbyn. In reality, the only certainty is that no one has the power to know the future. Within a year, we might all be gone. The "day when

---

141 Both the form and the *provenance* of this much-repeated quotation have often been disputed. It seems likely that Burke uttered something very like it and that others subsequently refined it

the inevitable asteroid slams into the earth and wipes [humans] out", to which Corbyn looked forward in a 2003 Commons motion, may have come by then[142]. But I plan to proceed as ever, braced for the worst, hoping for the best. We now have an unexpected player in the drama, an accidental hero to inspire us. And that, more than anything, lets me look forward to finding out what the future brings eagerly and with an optimistic heart.

---

142 Corbyn and John McDonnell seconded an Early Day Motion tabled by Tony Banks: "That this House is appalled, but barely surprised, at the revelations in MI5 files regarding the bizarre and inhumane proposals to use pigeons as flying bombs; recognises the important and life-saving role of carrier pigeons in two world wars and wonders at the lack of gratitude towards these gentle creatures; and believes that humans represent the most obscene, perverted, cruel, uncivilised and lethal species ever to inhabit the planet and looks forward to the day when the inevitable asteroid slams into the earth and wipes them out thus giving nature the opportunity to start again" [EDM 1255, May 21st 2004]

AFTERWORD to the SECOND EDITION:
ANTITHETICAL

Since the publication of the first edition of this book, the media's treatment of Jeremy Corbyn has been unprecedented in its vituperation, misrepresentation and selectivity. It began as it intended to go on. *The Huffington Post* reported analysis by the politically independent Media Reform Coalition of coverage of Corbyn's first week as Labour leader, a moment when in any other field (manager of the national football team, say, or chief conductor of the London Symphony Orchestra) judgment would be held in reserve and benefit of any doubt granted. The MRC collated 494 news reports, opinion columns and editorial leaders in the national press and found that 60 percent of these articles were clearly negative, 27 percent neutral and just 13 percent positive, despite the media's characterisation of Corbyn as an unknown quantity.

Predictably, *The Sun* and the *Daily Mail*, each with 91 percent, registered the highest proportion of stories that expressed hostility, animosity or unabashed ridicule. The report declared that the British press "systematically undermined" Corbyn, and concluded: "The risk of undue influence on elected politicians is high, and it's hard to see how democracy can flourish when the mass channels of debate are monopolised in the way that they are"[142].

If it were only the Tory press, one could account for it plainly. But the way the BBC too has treated Corbyn has been so consistently distorted that one must suspect an orchestrated stance required by the management in the belief that such a distortion will improve the Corporation's chances of surviving John Whittingdale's term as Culture Secretary. For example: presenter Mark Mardell referred in passing to Corbyn as "hard left" on Radio 4's *The World This Weekend*[143]. You can be sure that the BBC never refers to David Cameron as "hard right" or even "right wing" – he is after all "the Prime Minister", as Corbyn, you might think, is properly "the Leader of the Opposition". This is loaded terminology, intended (subconsciously or – let's be realistic – consciously) to put Corbyn beyond the consensual mainstream to which the BBC subscribes, to present him as "extreme".

Laura Kuenssberg, the BBC's political editor, interviewed Corbyn for the 6 pm bulletin on his view of regulations concerning police use of firearms and the so-called "shoot to kill" policy.

---

142 January 6th 2016
143 November 22nd 2015

It seemed to me that what Corbyn had to say was measured, judicious and sensible, the very antithesis of the gung-ho, trigger-happy mentality that animates some of the Tory backbenches. In her subsequent to-camera piece, Kuenssberg called Corbyn's view "extraordinary". Perhaps someone upstairs did find this gratuitous editorialising, for she did not repeat it on the 10 pm news[144].

Another needless thrust at Corbyn came in June Kelly's report on a court case: "... and it's emerged that one of the now convicted fraudsters, Mohamed Dahir, was supported by the Labour leader Jeremy Corbyn when he applied for and was given bail before the trial"[145]. This is malignly suggestive. The extended Dahir family are constituents of and known to Corbyn and, there being no grounds for him not to do so, he wrote in support of the bail application when Dahir was first charged. Dahir's lawyer only revealed this to the court after conviction, presumably in an attempt to leaven his client's sentence. Objectively, there is no justification for this titbit to be reported; that the case developed a (very tenuous) Syrian connection gave anyone wanting to smear Corbyn an innuendo with which to do so. Why the BBC should wish to do this remains unanswered. ITV's news bulletins

144 November 16th 2015
145 *6:00 News* BBC1 [December 10th 2015]

made no mention of the matter.

On December 3rd, less than three months into Corbyn's leadership and the day after the debate on Syria in the Commons, there was a by-election at Oldham West and Royton, following the death of Corbyn's great friend and ally Michael Meacher. The media expectation was that UKIP could well capture the seat. Its candidate had run Labour perilously close just over a year earlier at a by-election in the neighbouring constituency of Heywood and Middleton. The difficulty for the print media is that by-election results usually come too late for the next morning's deadline, as happened with Oldham. Guardian columnist Martin Kettle was so sure that Labour would get a bloody nose that, writing ahead but publishing later, he cited "a lousy by-election result in Oldham"[146].

In the event, Labour increased its vote share by a remarkable seven percent and the Tory vote dropped by nearly ten percent, only a small proportion of that change favouring UKIP. The media had to ditch their lovingly prepared editorials and think pieces declaring that the expected "lousy result" demonstrated once again the 'unelectability' of a party led by Corbyn. Curiously, they demurred at any notion that the actual result

---

146 December 4th 2015

indicated that any enthusiasm might attach to the leader.

The most astounding example of this double standard occurred on the BBC News report of the by-election result. So-called *vox pops* are used by lazy editors as news filler, purportedly to give a flavour of what 'ordinary people' think. There are two characteristics of the gambit that may readily be understood: first, views gathered in the street are random and unscientific and will usually demonstrate ignorance, indifference and scepticism, if not downright lunacy; second, if an editor wants to make a point, it may quickly be illustrated by finding people who are sufficiently excited at being 'on the telly' to make it for him.

In the BBC News report on the by-election, there was a succession of three local people, each of whom was bitterly scornful towards Corbyn[147]. Now it cannot be argued that no one could be found in the length and breadth of Oldham who would be prepared to say a good word for Corbyn's leadership. This is simple manipulation of the freedom of the airwaves to broadcast whatever the editor likes and call it news. And I will guarantee you this: if any research team ever looks into the BBC's record on by-election coverage, it will find

---

147 *6:00 News* BBC1 [December 4th 2015]

no news report before December 2015 in which all the views volunteered to the cameras rubbished the leadership of the party that had taken the seat, particularly when unexpectedly.

Laura Kuenssberg was at it again in reporting Corbyn's January 2016 reshuffle. There had been endless speculation about this in the media and a good deal of propaganda about 'revenge' and 'purges'. Again, no supportive reading would be afforded to whatever transpired. Corbyn would have proved himself a 'tyrant' or a 'Stalinist' had he sacked and/or moved frontbenchers who did not support his policies, 'powerless' and 'ineffectual' if he did not.

Kuennsberg was one of many commentators grumbling that the reshuffle was "so slow". There is no convention about the speed of reshuffles; they take as long as they take. They are, though, boring for reporters who have to wait around for developments. In this case, the days of media speculation long before Corbyn even began made it seem a more drawn-out affair. Furthermore, the process was hampered by various shadow ministers negotiating both publicly and privately, rather than following the usual practice of accepting the leader's prerogative and behaving in a dignified manner when they were moved or demoted (Maria Eagle was an honourable exception to this stricture).

Reporting the end of the reshuffle, Kuennsberg demonstrated a talent for superiority, belittlement, presumption and embroidery that chimed eerily harmoniously with David Cameron's thrusts at that morning's Prime Minister's Questions. As she had it: "[Corbyn] is meant to be the boss ... The leadership wanted [Hilary Benn] to move but he stayed put with a promise to work differently ... really? ... The last 24 hours have been a damaging pantomime. While Jeremy Corbyn's been bunkered up in his office with his close advisors, he hasn't always seemed in charge of events and simply he didn't have the clout to make all of the changes he wanted to"[148]. You, gentle reader, know as well as I do that Corbyn never told Kuennsberg the changes that he might have wanted to make or whether he wanted to move Benn from leading on foreign affairs, so her guess on this – it's just a guess – is no better than yours or mine. If she cannot perceive that phrases and terms like "meant to be the boss", "really?", "damaging pantomime", "bunkered up", "close advisors" (they are clearly meant to sound sinister, or why mention them?), "in charge of events" and "the clout" are the antithesis of

148 *6:00 News* BBC1 [January 6th 2016]

the scrupulous impartiality that the BBC charter obliges her to demonstrate, she may need a refresher course at the BBC academy.

Monitoring Kuenssberg on Twitter the previous day, Media Watch recorded her tweets about the issues of the week as: "Rail fares 0, Housing 0, Floods 1, EU negotiations 8, Labour reshuffle 30"[149]. Like everyone in the Westminster hothouse, her only interest is who's up and who's down, not what actually affects people's lives.

In the reshuffle, two ministers totally unknown outside their constituencies, Westminster and their families, Michael Dugher and Pat McFadden, were sacked. Both had been personally critical of Corbyn far beyond their respective ministerial briefs. At the time that Dugher was starting a tour of television studios making the most of his 'martyrdom', I put him into Google Search where his sacking was still only registering on its first page. Of 230 entries, just eight related to his work as Shadow Culture Secretary. That tells its own story. Dugher was immediately recruited as a columnist on *The Sun*, just as Simon Danczuk, another serial critic of Corbyn despite being a Labour MP, writes regularly in the *Daily Mail*. Why do these men gaily consort with the enemy? Do they imagine that such

---

149 Corbyn: Media Watch Facebook status [January 5th 2016]

newspapers would be devotedly supporting Labour if Liz Kendall were the Labour leader?

A small number of junior ministers, again peaking in public attention by so doing, resigned in the wake of these sackings. Unless they pick up lucrative contracts with the Tory press, we are unlikely to hear of them again (do tell me who it was who quit at the moment of Corbyn's election as leader, mentioned on page 101). One of the new quitters, Stephen Doughty (no, I haven't either), resigned with a live flourish on Andrew Neil's BBC magazine *Daily Politics*. Thanks to a blog by the BBC's so-called output editor[150], we know that the programme staff were in morning-long cahoots with anti-Corbyn Labour MPs and that this 'coup' was brokered by Laura Kuennsberg. Given that Cameron mentioned the resignation in PMQs before Corbyn knew of it, it can only be that the BBC gave the PM a heads-up: all highly improper.

Some people – those for instance who read *The Daily Telegraph* – imagine that the BBC is "full of pinkos". Far from it: the editor of BBC News is James Harding, a former editor of *The Times* (proprietor: Rupert Murdoch), a strong supporter of the Israeli government (and hence on that score at least at odds with Corbyn) and a "long-term friend"

---

150 Andrew Alexander, 'Resignation! Making the news on the *Daily Politics*' [BBC Academy website, January 7th 2016]

of George Osborne, towards whom *The Times* was notably kindly during Harding's tenure[151].

The executive editor of current affairs programming, including *Daily Politics*, is Robbie Gibb. He is brother to Tory Minister of State for Schools Nicolas Gibb, is a former chief-of-staff to Tory grandee Francis Maude, was best man at Tory businessman Mark MacGregor's wedding and was once deputy chair (to MacGregor) of the "extreme rightwing"[152] Federation of Conservative Students. So, no inclination to favour the Conservatives there, then.

It is hard to avoid the conviction that the media and the Blairite rump in the Labour Party are working together, either consciously or in an unarticulated understanding, to ensure that Corbyn's leadership does not survive until the 2020 election. The strategy is clearly to keep up a steady barrage of grumbling and nit-picking directed at Corbyn in the hope that he is forever in defensive mode, always doubted and questioned.

But this is a counsel of despair rather than a wise plan. It means to damage Corbyn but it has no means to prevent collateral damage to the Labour Party and to those of its adherents who like to be portrayed by the media as "the moderates"

---

151 according to *The Independent* [March 25th 2012]
152 according to *The Guardian* [July 14th 2015]

(which suggests sensible, realistic, virtuous, non-aggressive). The tactic can only be justified if it creates the opportunity for a challenge that has a prospect of achieving its goal and electing a 'vote-winning' leader. But four and a half years without such a challenge will make the Corbynistas dig in even more determinedly. Either way, it hardly promises a Labour victory in 2020. It is a grim prospect.

So I gently proffer the notion that those who support Corbyn start to prepare a Plan B. Instead of waiting for the likes of Chuka Umunna and Yvette Cooper and Rachel Reeves and Chris Leslie to gather round a rival candidate to challenge Corbyn (Hilary Benn, say, or David Miliband), let alone break away and form a new centrist party or join the Lib Dems or even the Tories, let them think about a new party of their own centred on Corbyn. It might be called the Democratic Socialist Party. The Socialist Party is a name already taken (led by Arthur Scargill) but no one would mistake Democratic Socialists for Social Democrats.

The party's policies would be undiluted Corbyn, so many of which are known to have a keen following in the country but are not yet embraced by any UK-wide party: getting rid of nuclear weapons, renationalising public transport and the public utilities, keeping the NHS wholly in public hands, changing economic direction to make the rich and the speculators support expansion and infrastructure and relieve poverty, re-energising enterprise that manufactures rather than merely services. There would be no need for a DSP to trim to the demands of the Blairites.

My guess is that there are about 25 sitting Labour MPs who might be prepared to resign the party whip *en masse* and stand for re-election as DSP candidates. Three of the most loyal Corbynistas are past 70 and might not want to start again; on the other hand, they might be all the more ready to fight one last time for a manifesto that they wholly support. Six of the MPs who loyally support Corbyn have majorities below 4,500; some of them might feel it's too risky to impose a by-election on their constituents.

But one of the great strengths of the Corbyn wing of the PLP is that so many have such healthy majorities – 14 of them are more than 10,000 votes ahead of their nearest rivals, including Corbyn, John McDonnell and Diane Abbott. The chances of them changing allegiance and taking their electorate with them must be at least as good as were those in the last parliament for the two Tories who got back in as UKIP MPs. Some 20 simultaneous by-elections would be very difficult for the Labour residuum to defend, especially with a (doubtless fraught) leadership election in prospect in a party suddenly light on its left wing; and those by-elections would be sprung at a time of the DSP's choosing.

In the months since the 2015 general election, the membership of the Labour Party has more than doubled. The number of those joining for the first time or rejoining after leaving during the Blair years now comfortably exceeds the entire membership of the Conservative Party. Those people were not brought in by Kendall, Cooper, Burnham or the prospect of Benn or the elder Miliband as leader. If the party countermands the democratic will of the quarter-million who voted for Corbyn, those people will have no reason to stay in the Party, and no reason to vote for it either.

If the Corbyn loyalists in the Commons saw that they had no choice but to break away and stand for re-election under new colours, a rump of 20-some-odd DSP MPs (two-and-a-half times as many as the Liberal Democrats) would be a solid basis for fighting a general election. I eschew predictions – a fool's game (or anyway a heedless columnist's game) – but I venture that there remains a strong chance of Corbyn being the next Prime Minister, though not necessarily as leader of the Labour Party.

Meanwhile the war of attrition grinds on. Though Corbyn may be tapping vast support in the country and the grassroots of the Party for his stances on not bombing targets in Syria and opposing the renewal of Trident missiles, there is an unwavering bloc in the PLP that will not be reconciled to these positions. It was perhaps a pious hope that Corbyn could hold such a divided party together by allowing diametrically opposed views to be expressed. Party management is always a fraught issue; for a leader with no experience of managing anything and little taste for compromise, it seems an insuperable task. But while this may look like a disaster up close, it is of little interest outside the Westminster hothouse.

It is in the constituencies and, with luck, in the non-party-joining wider world that Corbyn's appeal is working. At a December 2015 gathering of my own local party, it emerged that only six out of some 50 present had voted for Corbyn as leader in September, but there was now not a single member who identified as anti-Corbyn. "Give him a chance" is the very least enthusiastic endorsement that you hear, and that is enormously more generous than is granted by very many backbench Labour MPs. It is striking that it is the professional politicians who tend to take entrenched positions, their voters who are more willing to listen to contrary arguments and consider alternative strategies.

The babel of voices in the Labour movement is split into factions as well as, in cases like Simon Danczuk, conducting lone, self-advertising campaigns. From press coverage, you might imagine that there is just a single partisan grouping operating as an "enemy within", the much-maligned Momentum. On the contrary, there are quite as many groups of supporters who used to favour Tony Blair or Gordon Brown – the members that John Prescott has dubbed Bitterites – as there are those who would bury New Labour.

Progress, Labour Together, Labour First, Blue Labour and – this one known in Westminster as "the Resistance" – Labour for the Common Good are all ranged against Corbyn's leadership. Grassroots Alliance, Campaign Group, Tribune Group and Compass all lean relatively left. Socialist Campaign for a Labour Victory, Labour Representation Committee and Momentum are actively pro-Corbyn. There are also more than two dozen special interest groups that take stances on party policy.

Momentum is suspected most by the Bitterites because it is new, having grown out of Corbyn's leadership campaign, well-organised and diligent. During the fierce debate over extending RAF activity against Daesh into Syria, Momentum was accused of "bullying" Labour MPs who were inclined to support the government's call to legitimate the bombing. Anyone who uses social media knows that verbal abuse and even threats are made by supporters of every conceivable political position, that disobliging posts are nothing new and not confined to any single philosophy. Corbyn has regularly committed himself to avoiding personal attacks and called on his followers to do the same. But playing the martyr card is tempting for those who claim to have been verbally threatened, as if somehow their plight is comparable to (or even worse than) that of innocent Syrian citizens caught up in air raids. Tarring Momentum with the brush of brutality is mere propaganda, as is characterising it as the spawn of Militant Tendency, the entryist grouping that disrupted Neil Kinnock's leadership.

In fact Momentum is as broad church in its membership as the Party itself, united solely by the common experience of supporters being energised by Corbyn's honesty, courage and dissimilarity to the Westminster politicians fashioned from the traditional template. It is this support that gives Corbyn his power-base, rather than any significant presence in parliament. And it is a mighty power. Consider, for instance, the Facebook grouping called Corbyn 50yrs+ Supporters Group, set up to counter the notion that the Labour leader's constituency is dominated by callow, naïve and aggressive youngsters, an inevitability when Corbyn relies so much on the Internet (because, as we know, no one over 30 knows how to work a computer). When it first launched, membership of the group grew at the astonishing rate of more than 500 per day.

At about the same time, the Bitterites announced a drive to recruit 100,000 new "moderate" members to the Labour Party over eighteen months. They'll be lucky. Membership of the 50yrs+ group has stabilised at around 3,500, still a remarkable number. Had it been able to maintain its initial momentum, its strength would have topped 100,000 members in under seven months.

The enthusiasm for Corbyn out in the country gives a broad base upon which to build his restoration of Labour values. But popular support, I fear, may well be in vain. The world has changed since the Attlee government boldly transformed Britain. The powers ranged against governments and individual leaders are now much more entrenched, more ruthless, more subtle, better financed and better coordinated. Democracy is no match for vast wealth and remorseless self-interest.

In a wide-ranging analysis for the Strategic Culture Foundation, Finian Cunningham found that Jeremy Corbyn's then-imminent election as Labour leader revealed "just how undemocratic Britain is. Any politician who steps outside the establishment is liable for destruction by the ruling forces ... we can expect a full-on media war to destroy him over the next five years"[153]. Cunningham quoted the former British ambassador to Uzbekistan, Craig Murray: "Democracy in the United Kingdom is dysfunctional because an entrenched party system offers no choice ... The sheer panic gripping the London elite now is hilarious to behold"[154].

This is a salutary reminder that the civilised, tolerant and profoundly democratic reputation so complacently accorded to Britain by politicians is a very thin integument indeed. It can hardly be doubted that there is a force in the establishment both of Britain and of international capital that would have no intention of ever letting Corbyn anywhere near the seat of power.

153 'Labour's Corbyn: British Establishment in Destroy Mode' [August 20th 2015]
154 *ibid*

Consider the precedents. The stirrings of rebellion seriously arose during Harold Wilson's time as premier; in 1974, the army even briefly occupied Heathrow Airport, later claiming without much conviction that it was merely an unofficial training exercise. Wilson himself, inevitably accused of paranoia, remained convinced that elements in MI5 intended to remove him from office[155].

Exactly fifty years earlier, the Labour government of Ramsay MacDonald decisively lost the general election four days after the *Daily Mail* published the hugely damaging 'Zinoviev letter' which implied collusion between the British and Soviet governments to promote Marxist-Leninism in Britain, a letter that was subsequently found to be a forgery. Nobody was ever indicted for this assault on the democratic process. The history of dirty tricks, black propaganda and manipulation by sinister forces would certainly generate a new chapter if it seemed at all imminent that Corbyn were to be elevated by the electorate.

And since Corbyn became Labour leader, there has indeed been a disquieting matter around which some speculation swirls. His good friend Michael Meacher, MP for Oldham West and Royton, who had appeared in robust health, died unexpectedly after

---

155 see *The Pencourt File* by Barrie Penrose & Roger Courtiour [HarperCollins 1978]

a short illness the details of which have never been disclosed. Meacher once wrote a cogent analysis of the questions surrounding the 9/11 attacks[156] and reportedly had been lately taking renewed interest in the matter. Immediately following his death, the activist Tony Gosling tweeted: "Who deleted Michael Meacher's Twitter account? Surely not him or family – 6,341 tweets deleted – so who?"[157]. The on-line journal *Veterans Today* is among those that have questioned the innocence of his death[158].

But this is Europe, you will protest. Such things don't happen here. They only happen in South America. Or Africa; or the Middle East or the Far East ... or South Asia ... Nevertheless, democracy has been suspended, and draconian and murderous regimes installed, within living memory in European nations that we had thought were the absolute epitome of civilisation: Germany, Greece, Italy, Spain, Serbia and, to a lesser extent, Portugal. Those nations we now, in a different climate, think properly civilised again. But it would be foolish to believe that in Britain, where there is a widespread following for UKIP and much uglier movements than UKIP, popular support for such developments are unthinkable.

---

156 'This war on terrorism is bogus' [*The Guardian* September 6th 2003]
157 Tony Gosling Twitter account [October 21st 2015]
158 'Was British MP Michael Meacher murdered to cover up 9/11?' [veteranstoday.com October 24th 2015]

Eight days after Corbyn's election as Labour leader, *The Sunday Times* published remarks made on condition of anonymity by someone described as a senior serving general. "The general staff [of the Army] would not allow a Prime Minister to jeopardise the security of this country and I think people would use whatever means possible, fair or foul, to prevent that. You can't put a maverick in charge of a country's security. There would be mass resignations at all levels and you would face the very real prospect of an event which would effectively be a mutiny," he said[159].

There are many ways to read this. Given its non-attributability, it could have been cooked up in the editor's office – stranger things happen. Assuming it is authentic, it might have been an atypical blowhard – there have been many such in the senior ranks of the armed forces. It might have been a tactical move by a group of disaffected officers wishing to wrong-foot the Chief of the General Staff – as everywhere else, politicking goes on in the Army. It could have been Sir Nick Carter, the service's head honcho himself, funnelling his feelings through a trusted ally – top brass do not often make their opinions publicly known. Or it may just have been, yes, a senior serving general

159 September 20th 2015

shooting the breeze.

In the light of the *Sunday Times* piece, the polling organisation YouGov did some research. It found that a quarter of the British public could foresee a situation in which they would support a military coup in Britain. For almost ten percent, Corbyn becoming Prime Minister would constitute such a situation. If as PM Corbyn were to attempt to "dismantle" the armed forces, as many as 56 percent would support a coup. You might say defence cuts so far imposed by the Tories have "dismantled" in large measure.

What's more, 48 percent of UKIP voters believe the military should defy any civilian instruction that were considered unacceptable. I have not seen the wording of the questions nor the make-up of the sample taken, and I set no store by opinion polls of any kind; nonetheless, this should give pause. What clearly must be faced is that there are currents running at both a supranational and an anti-democratic level in preparation to pre-empt the kind of programme that Corbyn's supporters expect to elect him. In some scenarios, the ultimate weapon is unleashed to achieve this end. The pop singer Morrissey is widely held to be one of the more thoughtful and erudite individuals in his field. Playing a gig in Plymouth the week of

Corbyn's accession to the leadership, he told his audience: "You know he's a vegeterian? He doesn't like the monarchy? He hates war? They're gonna assassinate him"[160].

The challenge to the establishment that Corbyn represents is unprecedented. It seems heedless to rule out any eventuality. Does this then mean that it would be a kindness both to the nation and to Corbyn himself (and apologists like me) if he were to be persuaded to step back from leading Labour or some other party into the 2020 election?

Decidedly not. The movement he has sparked would never accept that solution. What Corbyn's elevation has already achieved is too inspiring to too many people for it to be abandoned without a fight to the last ditch, however vain it might appear. As Atticus Finch says in *To Kill a Mockingbird*: "Simply because we were licked a hundred years before we started is no reason for us not to try to win"[161]. Amen to that.

For an extended version of this afterword, see the author's blog at www.wstegcommonsense.blogspot.co.uk

160 *NME* [September 16th 2015]
161 Harper Lee 1960 [Penguin edition 1963 p 82]

INDEX

fn indicates a footnote

Over more than four decades,
W Stephen Gilbert has pursued
a highly varied career, having had
diverse books published, plays
produced on stage and television,
and reviews, reportage, columns and
essays published in a range of publications
on both sides of the Atlantic. He has edited
magazines, read scripts and pitched
screenplays in Hollywood.
In television, he script-edited *Minder*
and produced dramas including *Only
Connect* and *King of the Ghetto*. He
has served on boards, juries, panels
and advisory committees including
for Edinburgh, Locarno, the Bush and
BAFTA. But, like the Sondheim
character, he never does
anything twice.

ACKNOWLEDGMENTS

My editor and publisher Todd Swift took a leap
of faith with me comparable to that which the
Labour Party has taken with Jeremy Corbyn. He
has ensured I repaid it by always keeping me on
my toes. My esteemed Facebook friend Paul Ebbs
was instrumental in the connections being made.
My stalwart extra-digital friend Simon Farquhar
has consistently encouraged and badgered me for
longer than I can remember, but then he habitually
recalls the details of my life better than I do.

Martin Walker cast a beady professional eye
over the text to its great benefit. But all errors of
fact and apprehension are wholly my own. And
my beloved partner of 35 years, David James, has
patiently and thoughtfully sustained me through
the preoccupations of this undertaking. Without
him, I would achieve nothing.

◯◯ **EYEWEAR** PUBLISHING

we are an independent press
based in London, England.
Emphasis is on excellent new
work, in poetry and prose. Our
range is international and our
aim is true. Look into some of the
most stylish books around today.